Praise for Rachel S. Moore and

THE ARTIST'S COMPASS

"Rachel Moore has given artists—aspiring and those establishing themselves—a valuable gift in her book, *The Artist's Compass*. This is an insightful book filled with critical philosophical considerations about being an artist as well as work/life balance challenges and very basic but critical how-to information likes taxes, contracts, personal finances, and branding oneself."

—Dr. James Gandre, president of the
Manhattan School of Music

"Artists today must be as creative about their business as they are about their practice. Drawing on her experience as both an artist and an administrator, Rachel Moore has provided young artists with a no-nonsense handbook to success in today's entrepreneurial landscape."

—Deborah Borda, president and CEO of the
Los Angeles Philharmonic Association

"Rachel Moore is an inspiration as an artist and as a CEO. Her book is not just for performing artists, it's also essential reading for any young person looking for career advice and for anyone regardless of age on starting out on a new career path."

—Julia C. Levy, executive director of
Roundabout Theatre Company

"This is a truthful, pragmatic (and painful) approach to building a 'life' as an artist in today's world. Her style is concise and informative for anyone in the early stages of a career. I wish I had known all of this at twenty-five, since it took me until fifty to figure out most of these things!"

—Francesca Zambello, artistic and general director of the Glimmerglass Festival

"A wonderful resource—in fact, I wish it had been around when I was dancing. Moore offers so much practical advice for navigating a career in the performing arts, and I love that she also champions academic education."

—Amy Brandt, editor, *Pointe*

The
ARTIST'S
COMPASS

The Complete Guide to Building a Life
and a Living in the Performing Arts

RACHEL S. MOORE

President and CEO of The Music Center

TOUCHSTONE
New York   London   Toronto   Sydney   New Delhi

791
Moore
2016

Ｔ

Touchstone
An Imprint of Simon & Schuster, Inc.
1230 Avenue of the Americas
New York, NY 10020

First Touchstone trade paperback edition May 2017

TOUCHSTONE and colophon are registered trademarks of Simon & Schuster, Inc.

For information about special discounts for bulk purchases, please contact Simon & Schuster Special Sales at 1-866-506-1949 or business@simonandschuster.com.

The Simon & Schuster Speakers Bureau can bring authors to your live event. For more information or to book an event, contact the Simon & Schuster Speakers Bureau at 1-866-248-3049 or visit our website at www.simonspeakers.com.

Interior design by Jill Putorti

Manufactured in the United States of America

10 9 8 7 6 5 4 3 2 1

The Library of Congress has cataloged the hardcover edition as follows:

Names: Moore, Rachel, 1964–
Title: The artist's compass : the complete guide to building a life and a living in the
    performing arts / Rachel Moore, President and CEO of the Los
    Angeles Music Center.
Description: New York : Touchstone, 2016. | Includes bibliographical
    references and index.
Identifiers: LCCN 2015037025
Subjects: LCSH: Performing arts—Vocational guidance. | Performing
    arts—Economic aspects. | BISAC: BUSINESS & ECONOMICS / New Business
    Enterprises. | PERFORMING ARTS / Business Aspects. | SELF-HELP / Personal
    Growth / Success.
Classification: LCC PN1580 .M55 2016 | DDC 791.023—dc23 LC record available at
http://lccn.loc.gov/2015037025

ISBN 978-1-5011-0595-1
ISBN 978-1-5011-2664-2 (pbk)
ISBN 978-1-5011-0598-2 (ebook)

To my parents,
who encouraged me to dream

and

To my husband,
who helped me realize those dreams

There is a vitality, a life force, a quickening that is translated through you into action, and because there is only one of you in all time, this expression is unique.

And if you block it, it will never exist through any other medium and be lost. The world will not have it. It is not your business to determine how good it is, nor how valuable it is, nor how it compares with other expressions.

It is your business to keep it yours clearly and directly to keep the channel open. You do not even have to believe in yourself or your work. You have to keep open and aware directly to the urges that motivate you.

Keep the channel open. . . . No artist is pleased. [There is] no satisfaction whatever at any time. There is only a queer, divine dissatisfaction, a blessed unrest that keeps us marching and makes us more alive than the others.

—Martha Graham in conversation with Agnes de Mille,
from *Martha: The Life and Work of Martha Graham*

Contents

CONTENTS

Introduction

The life of the arts, far from being an interruption, a distraction, in the life of a nation, is very close to the center of a nation's purpose . . . and is a test of the quality of a nation's civilization.

—JOHN F. KENNEDY

Making a life and a living as a professional performing artist—what an extraordinarily rewarding, albeit challenging goal. Rewarding because it allows you to bring your unique voice to the world, challenging because it is fiercely competitive and constantly changing.

Given that you are reading this book, I'm going to assume that you are looking for practical, straightforward guidance to help you reach your goal. Whether you are currently studying to become a performing artist, have recently graduated from a performing arts conservatory, or are in the early stages of launching your career, this book will be your compass and provide you with the tools that will help you to navigate the business side of "showbiz"!

You may be a brilliant artist, but I want you also to become a savvy participant in the *business* of art. And, as I will be reminding you again and again, the arts are a business. As an example, American Ballet Theatre, for which I served as executive director/CEO from 2004 until 2015, has an annual operating budget of more than $43 million, the Music Center in Los Angeles has an annual operating budget of more than $65 million, and both organizations have hundreds of employees. These are definitely businesses.

First, let me assure you that I am absolutely sympathetic to the challenges you face, because I've been there. I've done it myself, and I know what it's like to enter a field that is extremely competitive, and where there seem to be no rules. The journey is energizing, terrifying, thrilling, heartbreaking, and always a compelling challenge. My purpose in writing this book is to provide you with information and ways of looking at things that will help you move forward in that dynamic and complex world.

So, who exactly am I to be making these claims? I am currently the president and CEO of The Music Center in Los Angeles, a venue similar to Lincoln Center in New York. I oversee the theaters where the Los Angeles Philharmonic Orchestra, the Center Theatre Group, the Los Angeles Master Chorale, and the Los Angeles Opera perform, and I also oversee all the dance and the Center's education programming as well as the programming for the city's Grand Park.

Previously, as I've said, I served as CEO of American Ballet Theatre, one of the world's premier ballet companies, which I originally entered as a performer.

I grew up in Davis, California, which is a small college town, home to the University of California, Davis. When I was eleven, a friend and I signed up for a ballet class at the Davis Arts Center just because we thought it would be a fun thing to do. And it turned out that not only did I love it, I was also very good at it. When I was thirteen, the Joffrey Ballet came to Davis, and I was offered a scholarship to join the company's summer program in New York. I thought I was ready for the big city, but my parents, in their wisdom, didn't think it would be appropriate for a thirteen-year-old girl to spend the summer in New York, essentially on her own. The next summer, however, they allowed me to participate in a program in Carlisle, Pennsylvania, that my ballet teacher had found for me. It was a good program, it was a safe environment, and I had a great time.

I finally went to New York when I was fifteen, spending the summer at the School of American Ballet, the official school of New York City Ballet. The following year my summer studies continued with American Ballet Theatre (ABT), and then, when I was seventeen, I was offered a scholarship to become a full-time student at ABT. By then I thought I'd reached the heights of sophistication, but I was really still a pretty naïve teenager from a small California town. My parents said that before I moved away and started studying ballet on a full-time basis, I had to finish high school and I also had to get good grades. Naturally, I thought my life was completely over. Dancing was my passion. It was all I wanted to do, and I was sure that I'd never get another chance to fulfill that dream of performing with a major ballet company—all because of my parents.

Looking back, and knowing what I know now, I realize how lucky I am to have had parents who not only valued education but also were, of all things, professional economists who modeled for me the essential elements of personal financial responsibility. The following year, when I was eighteen and invited to join the company, I realized that, of course, my life wasn't ruined after all. Not only would I have my chance, but it would be grounded and strengthened by completing my high school education, which also meant leaving the door open to pursue higher education later.

Appreciating this now as I couldn't at the time, I have made it a point as an executive in the arts world to actively encourage students to take their academic education seriously and to complete as much formal education as is possible within their chosen performance field. ABT, for one, no longer hires anyone under the age of eighteen to be part of the professional company. The rationale is, if you are talented at sixteen, you will likely be talented (and that much better trained) at eighteen, and at eighteen you will also have a more complete education and greater emotional maturity to cope with the competitive and extremely intense world of professional ballet.

With hindsight, I see that my parents, whose view back then was much longer than mine, didn't want me to close any doors to my future, which I surely would have done if I'd left high school without a diploma. That decision turned out to be more important than any of us could have imagined when injury brought my dancing career to a premature halt at the age of twenty-four. Because I'd finished high school with good grades, I was able to shift gears, return to school, earn a BA from Brown University, a master's degree in arts administration from Columbia University, and reenter the world of performing arts in a series of administrative positions.

I tell you all this because I want you to understand that, whatever you've experienced or may need to navigate as you launch your career, I've either been through it myself or I know someone who has. Yes, my personal experience has been in the world of ballet, but whether you're a dancer, a singer, a classical musician, or an actor, you are a performing artist, which means that you are hoping to make a successful career in a tough, competitive world—one where only a few have the luxury of belonging to an established organization that offers even a modicum of support or the promise of a regular paycheck.

Indeed, the chances of a young performer being able to move directly from a major conservatory or university program into a job with a major orchestra, dance, or theater company are, today, almost nonexistent. While that used to be the common road to career advancement, it is no longer. I don't want to sound harsh, but it's important to face the facts. There are many ways in which the performing arts world has changed, but one of the most significant for you is that, quite simply, there are not as many full-time jobs as there were thirty years ago. Orchestras and opera companies across the country are in financial difficulty and have either closed their doors or are reducing the number of musicians in their orchestras in order to survive. Even the extremely highly regarded New York City Opera was forced to close in 2013—after seventy years—because it could not make ends meet.

The causes of the challenges facing the nonprofit performing arts are many and varied—including the fact that audiences for live performances are aging, while younger, more technologically savvy consumers of the arts are often less interested in traditional, proscenium-based performances. The result is that the world has changed and continues to change drastically for emerging artists. But that doesn't mean the performing arts world is fading; it only means that the ways in which we practice our craft and share it with audiences are evolving. Because of that, performing artists in the twenty-first century must be more entrepreneurial and marketing-savvy than their peers of the past. But this actually is a great boon to today's performers. With all the connectivity and digital resources available, performers now have a multitude of ways to learn, network, self-promote, and find out how they can forge their own path so that their unique voice can be heard.

This book aims to help you with that journey. Up till now, it is likely that you have had significant training in your art form. You have had teachers who have served as your mentors and your greatest cheerleaders. They want nothing more than for you to succeed as an artist. And they've been doing everything in their power to help you do that. But, as I've learned through my own experiences as a performer and an arts administrator, most teachers who are expert in their respective artistic disciplines are not necessarily expert in the *business* of the performing arts.

In recent years, I've spoken with many dance and music teachers about the likelihood of their students' getting jobs. All of them were deeply passionate about wanting the absolute best for their students, but as we spoke it became quite clear to me that most of them had no idea how limited the opportunities actually are, and virtually none had any understanding of the degree to which technology is changing the performing arts. In fact, several of the older, highly regarded teachers looked at me with horror written all over their faces when I mentioned the idea of artists having a "brand." One had no idea what Twitter was or how it worked.

While I truly appreciate and understand these teachers' devotion to their students and their art, I also understand that many, if not most of them, are not equipped to help emerging performers navigate the arts world as it exists today outside of the studio.

Once you emerge from the protection of a school, college, or conservatory program, you are effectively on your own. The competition is fierce, and while the people who hire you naturally want you to succeed, it's mainly because their own success depends on yours. Distressing as it might seem to you now, the performing arts is, at root, a business, and you will need to embrace that notion in order to make smart career decisions. The reality is that if you can't cut it, you'll get cut—from the show or the corps or the orchestra. And if the production ends or never takes off, even if you, personally, are brilliant, you'll still be out of work, and you'll need to figure out how to survive without starving until the next opportunity comes along.

So, at the same time you're learning to navigate your way through the professional performing world as an artist, you're also having to learn all kinds of new work/life skills—from signing contracts for gigs to managing a budget, getting insurance, and—if, like the majority of performing artists, you don't have a single full-time employer—paying estimated taxes, among many other responsibilities.

While this may sound daunting and scary, I absolutely don't want to discourage you from moving forward with your career. Why? *Because the world needs you!* We all need people in the performing arts—to create beauty, to allow us to see the world in new and different ways, to challenge our assumptions, and to spark creativity in the audiences of today and tomorrow. Those who dedicate themselves to the arts strive every day to make the world a better place. This is a noble and worthy cause to embrace, but certainly not an easy one to pursue. The journey is worth the effort, but you need to be strategic and work "smart," not just "hard."

My goal is to encourage you, and to help you carve out a life that allows you to put yourself forward, pursue your dream, and enjoy a long and successful career without the attendant anxiety that comes from constantly living on the economic edge.

In the chapters that follow you'll be reading about various young artists who have managed to jump-start careers, pumping up both their image and their income by taking advantage of the artistic business opportunities offered outside the traditional models. So please, don't dismiss the business side of the arts. Once upon a time, artists could say, "Hey, I'm an artist; I don't need to know anything about business." But that is no longer true. The performing arts world is increasingly focused on business, and if you are to thrive in that world, or even just survive, it must be your business to know about the business you're in, and I'm making it my business to help ensure that you do.

To begin, we're going to sit down and figure out who you are as an artist, what you believe makes your work different or special, what kind of career you envision for yourself in the future, and, perhaps, what kind of career may suit you best. There's a good reason why the phrase "know thyself" was written in stone in the forecourt of the Temple at Delphi by ancient Greek philosophers and wise men. If you don't know who you are—and who you wish to become—you are, in effect, operating in the dark without a flashlight, sailing off into the unknown without a map or a compass. So let's dive in and help you find a sense of direction.

Chapter One

What Does Success Look Like to You?

Assessing Your Goals and Strengths as an Artist

> It is necessary . . . for a man to go away by himself . . .
> to sit on a rock . . . and ask of himself, "Who am I, where have I been,
> and where am I going?"
>
> —CARL SANDBURG

I love speaking to students about career development, but I've found that whenever I ask what they intend to do after graduation, even the most gifted among them get that deer-in-the-headlights expression in their eyes and draw a complete blank.

Why is this such a tough question for so many young artists to answer? I think it's because so many of their waking hours are spent focusing on the details—the exact movement of an arm, the precise fingering of a complex musical passage, the exact inflection of a monologue—that they can lose sight of the big picture: Why am I doing all this hard work, anyway? And what is it that I hope to achieve? What, after all is said and done, does success look like for me?

Let's face it, most performing artists spend a lot of time comparing themselves to others in one way or another—physical appearance, intelligence, professional skills, personality, ambition (or lack thereof), and talent. While these sorts of comparisons may be relatively common, I would venture to say that they are particularly poisonous for those in the performing arts.

Don't get me wrong. Self-assessment is not a bad thing. In fact, it's absolutely necessary, so long as it's objective and realistic. Why? Because if we are truly aware of who we are and how we stack up against others in our field, we will be better prepared to define what it is that makes us unique and, therefore, to project that image to the world and make it work to our advantage.

The problem is that, for those in the performing arts, this process is especially complicated: For one thing, assuming you've achieved a certain level of proficiency in your chosen field, there is really no objective standard against which to measure any one person's artistry. And because that judgment is subjective at best, what differentiates you from your peers becomes more about style and personality, or what is generally referred to as "voice," than about actual skill level. Your unique voice is ultimately going to be the thing that sets you apart and becomes your artistic calling card. In marketing terms, it will be your *brand*.

As a student of the performing arts, you are schooled to take correction and pursue a virtually unattainable level of perfection, and so your opinion of your own skill level may be skewed by an overdeveloped inner critic or an underdeveloped trust in your own achievements. But demeaning your own abilities in the service of self-assessment or seeming humility is neither helpful nor constructive. As a very wise teacher once said to me, "If you constantly put yourself down—even if you don't particularly believe it—you will end up believing it. How you describe yourself to others and yourself is extremely powerful, so be fair about your strengths and weaknesses, but don't start beating yourself up—you will get nowhere."

Two basic truths I've discovered in the course of my own career as well as in the careers of those whom I've mentored and overseen for the last few decades are:

1. In order to be truly happy in your career, you need to define success for yourself rather than letting others define it for you.

2. The key to success in the arts (no matter how you define it) is, in the end, a matter of identifying and following your unique voice as a performer.

DEFINING YOUR VOICE

So what is your voice—your unique personality, perspective, and way of expressing your particular art? You need to value your voice, your particular contribution, figure out how it fits into the changing world of the performing arts, and find a way for that voice to be heard. What is it that you want to say to the world? What special thing do you have to contribute to your art? For me it was being able to feel the music and use what I felt to bring something personal and special to my performance through timing, expression, and technique.

Whenever I see a group of young dancers in a classroom, all of whom are on approximately the same level, I look for the one who has an internal perspective that brings something special to everything he or she does. It could be the way she uses her arms, her timing, the way he looks up and out that projects confidence in his performance, or the fact that, when there's room for interpretation, she makes an interesting and elegant choice—not simply to stand out, but always in service of the art. In fact, I believe that in most instances, those who stand out, especially at a young age, make those choices unconsciously, as an organic expression of who they are. The truth of this was brought home to me once again as I recently watched a video showing a class of kids dancing to Mark Ronson and Bruno Mars's "Uptown Funk." Right in the middle of the front row was a tiny eight-year-old—the smallest kid in the group—who was hitting each movement with an energy that just screamed "Watch me!" That kid had *attitude,* but he also had the coordination and the talent to back it up.

The same was true when I was running a classical music school in Boston. There were always those kids who had a really good ear and were technically advanced—and then there were the ones who would actually bring magic to their music. One of them was Tony Rymer, a little boy with a big smile who wanted to be a cellist. It was clear from the moment he walked onto the stage as a second grader that Tony had a gift. His eyes sparkled while he played, his technical skills came naturally, his sound was warm and true, and his performance radiated with an inner confidence. Tony went on to graduate from the New England Conservatory of Music and is now a professional cellist. He has won numerous competitions and performed major concerti to critical acclaim with the Atlanta Symphony, the Boston Pops, the Cleveland Orchestra, and the Detroit Symphony.

As a young performer you need to figure out what you have to contribute to the world, why you do certain things in a certain way, and why you think they are beautiful or special or compelling. If you don't think you have something special to bring to your art, I'd have to say that you probably shouldn't be doing this. It's too hard, and those who are successful are the ones who can't imagine doing anything else because they have something they need to say.

One experience I'll never forget occurred when I was dancing in the corps at ABT and the great Russian ballerina Natalia Makarova came to stage a production of *La Bayadère,* an ornate tale of love and revenge set in royal India. In Act II, the warrior Solor is grief-stricken by the murder of his true love, Nikiya, a temple dancer.

In a sequence known as "Kingdom of the Shades," Solor has an opium-induced dream during which he encounters twenty-four "shades" who are exact likenesses of Nikiya. The shades, corps members in white tutus, enter one by one, each making precisely the same sequence of slow, sustained movements as the dancer before her, until the stage is filled with row upon row of silent figures moving in complete synchrony. Incredibly beautiful; incredibly difficult.

When Makarova came into the room to stage that sequence, I'd guess that all twenty-four of us young shades were terrified. What she told us then was truly an "aha" moment for me: "Each one of you is a princess unto yourself. I want to see each one of you. You're special and beautiful. You're not just a row of Nikiyas."

"Okay," I thought. "I'm in a line with twenty-three other dancers and we're all doing the same thing. How can I make this special and beautiful unto myself?" I felt as if I'd just been given permission to interpret the movements and bring my own voice to the stage. That was a great gift, but it also came with great responsibility—not simply to follow direction but to think creatively about each movement and put my stamp on everything I did, be it through my unique musicality or a particular physical inflection.

Part of what it means to be an artist—whether you're a dancer or a singer or a musician—is finding a way to be individual even when you're doing the same thing as everyone else. It's something every young artist must figure out for him- or herself, both to be competitive at an audition and to bring value to his or her work, whether it is as the lead in a theatrical production, in the chorus of an opera company, part of a musical ensemble, or a member of the *corps de ballet,* as I was in *La Bayadère.* Whatever your role, however big or small, you will have the opportunity to work with other amazing artists and create beauty on the stage. And, if you are lucky, you will be part of an established group that provides steady employment and organizational support (as opposed to gigging as a freelance artist your entire life), but first you need to project your own special voice so that you stand out from the crowd and get the job.

So, how will *you* define success as an artist? What is the unique brand you want to bring to the world? These are questions that all performers must ask themselves, both at the beginning of their careers, and again at various points moving forward, in order to figure out their artistic mission or purpose and define their priorities as well as their personal and professional strengths. In the words of universally acclaimed, award-winning actress Sigourney Weaver, "It takes a lot of communing with oneself to recognize what you have accomplished and get a clear idea of what you want to do."

Thinking honestly about these tough questions is the first step toward building a fulfilling career and an equally fulfilling life. For some of you that will mean a life of performing. For others it could mean playing any one of a variety of roles within the business of the performing arts.

DEFINING YOUR BRAND

There could be an endless number of attributes that go into determining who you are, but when it comes to branding yourself as an artist, it's important to really understand what makes you different and what you bring to the field, and then be as clear and concise as possible about how you express that. If you're wondering how to do it, think in terms of what someone else might say about you if your name came up in a conversation about casting a particular role, or if he were recommending you for a job. To help you figure it out, think of your brand as comprising two distinct sets of attributes—the rational and the emotional.

1. **Rational Attributes**: These are the specific areas of expertise you bring to the position: What is your unique artistic contribution? What skills do you have? What special professional strengths do you bring to the production to ensure its success? What previous experience do you have that will contribute to

your future performance? Directors of companies frequently share notes about performers with one another, and I've often heard leaders of performing arts organizations talk about an artist who "can command the stage," "is technically brilliant," or is "incredible at supporting roles." These are the hard-core skills that get you into the game. Without them, you won't be considered. Think of them as "necessary but not sufficient" for success.

2. Emotional Attributes: These attributes describe the "softer," more personal side of your brand. What is your personality type; your style of interaction; your ability to work in a team; your level of likability, trustworthiness, and reliability? Emotional attributes are the personality characteristics and life experiences that make you interesting and different. Added to your rational attributes, they can either help or hinder your ability to connect with people. There are artists who are absolutely brilliant onstage whom no one will hire because of their bad attitude, their unreliability, or their refusal to work with a director, preferring to do things "their own way."

Taken together, your rational and emotional attributes define what you have that is unique in the marketplace, what makes you special and worth hiring, and thus what is your personal brand.

So let's take a moment to figure out your own rational and emotional attributes.

On a piece of paper, write down these four aspects of what makes each of us unique.

* **Core values.** These are the aspects of your character that describe who you are deep down and what values

you hold dear. Examples might include thoughtfulness, trustworthiness, courage, respect, integrity, being honest, being open, helping others, or being reliable.

* **Artistic strengths.** These might include extreme musicality; an ability with accents, learning scores, ballets, or scripts quickly; the ability to transform the prosaic into something original; stage presence; adaptability; vision; technical skills; the ability to take criticism; creative problem solving; being collaborative, imaginative, a good communicator.
* **Personality.** These attributes describe how you interact with the world and are perceived by others. For example: being positive, creative, strategic, focused, confident, friendly, energetic, patient, flexible, passionate, unflappable, having a sense of humor.
* **Image.** This is the image you project to others based on your personal look or style or language. Such as: sophisticated, elegant, edgy, classic, hip, cultured, chic, sexy, urbane.

Now, write down the words you would use to describe yourself in each of these categories. You may want to enlist a friend or a colleague to help you figure out how others see you—and to keep you honest. Simply tell them you need help with a branding exercise and ask them to describe you candidly and honestly.

Once you have a list, try to figure out how to link these attributes to one another. How your personal qualities fit together will be key to determining who you are and developing your brand.

For instance, are you a visionary artist who can work with

anyone? Or are you a master technician who is completely reliable and can be counted on to perform in any situation? If, for example, someone asks you what you do, don't just say, "I'm a violinist." Instead you might say, "I'm a classical violinist with a focus on integrating new technology into my work so that it is more accessible to others," or, "I'm a choreographer, and I am working on ways to create narrative works using a new dance vocabulary." My own tagline is that I like to see myself as an entrepreneurial leader. Regardless of the specifics, think about how you would quickly and succinctly capture yourself in a personal tagline.

Now that you have a sense of how you see yourself and how others see you, you can craft a personal "message" to help you communicate your brand to potential employers, colleagues, audience members, patrons, and the broader public.

DEFINING YOUR MISSION
OR PURPOSE AS AN ARTIST

Artists are mission- or goal-driven. Some even regard their work as a calling. They feel they have something special to add to the world and thus they are willing to work tirelessly and overcome great challenges in order to make their personal artistic contribution. In my philosophy classes at Brown, the professors used to say that when you are justifying an argument, you need to meet the "Oh yeah?" and "So what?" challenges. By this they meant that you need to explain "oh yeah?" or "Why do you think this is right? How are you justifying your claim?" But even if you are able to do that, it isn't enough. You also need to explain why anyone should care, thus answering the question, "So what?"

Both Andrew Simonet, founder and director of Artists U, and Susan Mohini Kane, a classical soprano and voice teacher, suggest that crafting an "Artist's Mission Statement" will help emerging performers articulate both for themselves and for others the reason(s) they exist as artists. This statement must be clear and based on personal beliefs and values.

Consider the following questions and jot down your answers, as you may want to return to them again and again.

Why is your work significant or essential to you? What is it that makes you passionate about your work? For me, it was believing that, through dance, I was creating moments of great beauty that spoke of what I thought was true in the world. I thought this would help to change the way people saw the world, and, consequently, help to change the world.

Beyond your own personal interest or benefit, why should your work matter to others? Why do you think people connect to it and care about it? How is it different from others' and why is that important? Keep in mind that you are in a performing art form, where the audience's relationship to your work is critical, so this question must be answered compellingly. This will probably be difficult for you to articulate, but it is essential that you figure it out if you are ever going to differentiate yourself from the crowd and engage a substantial audience.

WHERE ARE YOU NOW?

How you assess yourself and chart your course moving forward will depend on where you are right now.

If you're just at the beginning of your journey and have not yet graduated from high school, you and your parents need to discuss your plans for getting your diploma. As I found out for myself, it's important to keep your options open. Anything can happen to any one of us at any time. You may need or want to change your career course and do something entirely different, even if you can't imagine such a thing at this point in your life. Therefore, you need to figure out how you can pursue your arts training while still keeping up academically. For example, look into the various summer programs available to you and check out those options.

If you're at the point of applying to a conservatory or a college-level performing arts program, consider whether the schools you're applying to offer classes that will help you prepare for the professional world you're hoping to enter, such as courses in the business of the performing arts or career planning. If you have some idea of what you're going to do with your training before you have to enter the job market, you'll be that much ahead of the game (which is exactly why I'm writing this book in the first place).

If you're past the point of applying and are now attending or have recently graduated from a professional training school, it's time to think about why you are so committed to performing. What is it that compels you to pursue your chosen art form? What particular skills do you bring to the professional table?

What is it that makes you stand out in the ever-changing world of the performing arts business?

WHERE DO YOU GO FROM HERE . . .
AND HOW DO YOU GET THERE?

If we're being honest, I'm sure we're all aware, at least to some degree, that we're better at some things than others, and the things we're good at are generally also the things we love most. Knowing where you excel will certainly help you to find your particular niche in the marketplace—and, in all probability, the jobs you most enjoy—but it's still necessary to reach a certain level of expertise in every aspect of your field in order to be competitive. If you want to pursue a career in musical theater, for example, it's important to sing and act well, but if you can also dance well, you'll be that much more likely to get hired.

I should also make it clear at this point that being multi-talented does not in any way mean you shouldn't home in on the particular strength that guides and infuses everything you do. All it means is that you'll have more outlets for expression while developing other marketable skills. I can think of no two better examples to illustrate this important point than the careers of Jerome Robbins and Leonard Bernstein, both of whom excelled (often in collaboration) in the worlds of both the popular and classical aspects of their fields. During his time as a classical ballet dancer (a soloist with ABT from 1941 to 1944) and choreographer (most notably with New York City

Ballet), he was also producing, directing, and choreographing Broadway and Hollywood musicals. In 1944 he conceived and choreographed the original Broadway production of *On the Town*, for which Bernstein wrote the music. In 1957, the year Leonard Bernstein was appointed music director of the New York Philharmonic, a position he held until 1969, the two collaborated again, this time on creating, writing, and producing *West Side Story*. I feel it is safe to say that no one familiar with their work would ever question the fact that each of these multitalented stars of their chosen fields brought an extremely strong, consistent, and uniquely identifiable voice to each and every one of his endeavors. And their spirit of collaboration and diversification goes on: several dancers from New York City Ballet as well as American Ballet Theatre principal dancer Misty Copeland have appeared in the recent Broadway revival of *On the Town*, and Christopher Wheeldon, a well-known ballet choreographer, is directing the Broadway production of *An American in Paris*.

Cenovia Cummins, a classical violinist, is currently the concertmaster of the New York Pops, Riverside Symphony, and the School of American Ballet Orchestra. She is also an active chamber musician, having played with the Chamber Music Society of Lincoln Center, and the Grand Canyon and Moab music festivals. And she has played backup for popular singers ranging from Tony Bennett to P. Diddy, and Barbra Streisand to Rod Stewart. She is the poster child for entrepreneurial diversification and offers this advice to other young artists:

1. Educate yourself about the world. It makes for a better artist.
2. Try to diversify yourself. [In addition to the violin, Cenovia plays the viola, mandolin, piano, and guitar.]
3. Be flexible; don't automatically say no to a gig that you think is beneath you. You may meet people and it may open opportunities you didn't know existed.
4. Always be positive. People are attracted to positive energy. Even if you don't feel terribly positive, put on a positive front.
5. Always try to be the best version of the person you want to be.

Like artists themselves, the arts industry as a whole is, of necessity, evolving to be more open and flexible in order to attract new and diverse audiences. The Music Center, for one, is always seeking to work with artists who are forward-looking, able to collaborate with a variety of art forms, and use technology in new and interesting ways. If an artist can do something that is unique and relevant to twenty-first-century audiences, performing arts organizations of all types will be open to hiring that person.

Any real artist will want to improve all their skills all the time, just because they want to get better at what they do. But being an "all around" performer and being open to trying new things will also make you a more marketable one, helping you to build new connections and create more performance opportunities.

More and more often, in order to broaden their audiences, classical venues and productions are partnering with popular artists and popular music. The New York Philharmonic has performed an extremely well-received concert featuring the music from *Star Wars*, and in the winter of 2015 Renée Fleming, the renowned American-born operatic soprano, was joined by Broadway singer Kelli O'Hara in a production of Franz Lehár's *The Merry Widow* at the Metropolitan Opera. Boundaries between the so-called high and low arts are fast disappearing, and it's becoming more important than ever for performers to focus on what is beautiful and fulfilling, wherever that is found.

A Word About Career Choices

"I rebelled against a 'golden age' model that set specific repertoire, and a specific career path that great singers of previous generations had followed. I was more interested in singing lesser-known roles, and I wanted to branch out stylistically. That 'golden age' template was very much a European model. As an American-born and raised singer, I needed to incorporate my own taste and sensibility, which include the popular genres that I had listened to growing up. . . . I believe a broader approach to musicianship is increasingly important for young performers. Singers today need to be prepared to learn quickly, perform new music, and cultivate the artistic flexibility to embrace nontraditional styles of performance and theatrical skills. [But n]one of this is a substitute for hard technical work, and the development of one's artistry, style, language, audition techniques, and the vast body of knowledge that underlies the classical music tradition."

—Renée Fleming

In addition to developing and broadening your technical skill set, however, you also need to work on mastering mental toughness and developing a realistic sense of what is possible for you. I remember seeing a T-shirt years ago that said, "Tough but Fair," and that's how you need to be with yourself. You may not ever be able to do everything you wish you could, but you do need to develop the skills you have to the highest degree of which you are capable. And if you wish you could do something (jump higher, hit a higher—or lower—note, cry on cue) as well as somebody else, remember that he or she is probably just as envious of something you can do better. We are not, after all, just "a row of Nikiyas."

The problem is that most of us want to do the things we're good at and have to push ourselves to do what makes us uncomfortable. A perfect example of someone who understood this is David Hallberg, a principal dancer with ABT who joined the Bolshoi Ballet in Moscow as a *premier danseur* in 2011 and now splits his season between the two. His reasons were twofold: there was a particular Bolshoi coach he wanted to work with, and he also felt that he wanted to learn more about the unique style of the Bolshoi Ballet and to work on his jumps, an area for which the Bolshoi is world renowned.

Not everyone will have the wherewithal to go off and do this on their own, but there is help out there for those who may have the will but not the means. For example, there are many exchange programs that allow young performers to experience what it's like to work with different organizations in different venues. And organizations such as the Annenberg Foundation give grants to help midcareer artists get the additional training that will, in effect, fill the gaps in their skills and help them move to the next level. Keep that in mind; we'll be discussing these possibilities in greater detail in Chapter 6.

When I was in the process of changing careers, one of the best pieces of advice I received was from an executive recruiter who told me, in essence, "If you want to get a top job in arts management, you need to take a good hard look at your résumé, figure out where the gaps are, and pursue jobs that will help you fill those gaps." Consider the advice and stories you've just read and ask yourself: Are there aspects of your art or professional skill set that you could develop in order to make you a more marketable performer?

In years past, there were many large companies willing to invest in the development of young artists with talent, but those are fast disappearing, and it is becoming more and more important for emerging artists to become self-starters and create their own opportunities. The incubators for developing artists may be largely gone, but so are the gatekeepers, which means that anyone can create their own opportunities if they're clever enough, determined enough, and talented enough to assess the marketplace and take advantage of what's out there. In Chapter 3 we're going to be talking in detail about how you can create those opportunities for yourself. For now, I just want you to consider that self-marketing as well as self-development are going to be critical to how you get from where you are to where you want to be in your career as a performing artist.

HOW DO YOU DEAL WITH CHANGE?

With a few daredevil exceptions, most of us humans don't really like change. We like to know what's going to happen; we like to have a routine. As a student, you probably knew pretty much how each day was going to go for you—so many hours of class; so many hours of practice. Get up and go to bed in the same place at the same time every day. As a professional, however, things are likely to be a lot less predictable, particularly as the world of the performing arts is evolving today. In Chapter 2 we'll be talking a lot more about those changes and how some artists are using them to their advantage, but the bottom line is that technology is fast changing the face of what we have always thought of as the classical arts.

There are fewer and fewer "permanent jobs" to be had in any discipline, and except for those few of you who become members of an orchestra, a ballet, an opera, or a repertory theater company, you'll be working many different gigs (if you're lucky) or at least trying out for many different jobs that could last for a few weeks or a few months, or just a couple of days. And that doesn't even include the jobs you thought would last at least a few months that crashed and burned almost at once. But even within a company it is not uncommon for a performer to play at least two different roles in different vehicles in the course of a single day. Even more likely, however, is that, as a freelancer you will "gig" in multiple jobs in a single day. There are, for example, many musicians who substitute in pit orchestras on Broadway, in which case a single musician could easily play in one show for the matinee, in another for the evening performance, and then in a third show for the matinee the following day.

Change has always been a constant in the performing arts, but this is truer now than ever before. The goal is to acknowledge that fact and make it work to your advantage. If you can't, or if you stubbornly refuse to adapt, you will simply get left behind. More and more, the successful artist is the one who is constantly looking forward, saying, "I see things changing. I need to be proactive; I have to find a way to be the master of my fate and figure out how I am going to fit into the future." Adam Shankman, director, choreographer, and Hollywood producer, reframed his artistic skills by capitalizing on the creation of music videos and the increased use of popular dance in movies and TV shows. A former Juilliard student, Shankman started his career by dancing in music videos with Paula Abdul and Janet Jackson before moving on to choreograph numerous films. He has also directed movies and television programs including *Hairspray,* the film adaptation of the Broadway musical *Rock of Ages,* and multiple episodes of *Glee.*

As with many things in life, when you come up against a barrier, you need to find a way to get over it or around it rather than stamping your foot in frustration and saying it isn't fair that the barrier exists. You can't simply dig in your heels and demand that the world adapt to your way of doing things. That's just not happening, and it's why technological change is so scary for so many people. It's important to get into a mindset that makes you receptive to change and allows you to embrace it as a welcome challenge and an opportunity to grow.

In the world of opera, the introduction of high-definition broadcasts of performances to theaters across the globe has proved to be a difficult transition for some singers, who have had to become more aware of their physical appearance (those close-ups can be tough) and both willing and able to participate in live interviews during the intermissions. Those artists who have adapted and embraced this new way of distributing opera will be more successful as professionals today and tomorrow.

HOW WILLING ARE YOU TO TAKE RISKS?

If you're resistant to change, and if you find yourself extremely anxious and ill each time you have to go onstage, it's safe to say that you really don't like taking risks. Getting ahead in any business—and that includes the performing arts—often means taking calculated risks. If you're not willing to take on the challenge of trying something new when the opportunity presents itself, you may find yourself doing the same thing over and over. That may be what works for you, and it's okay, so long as you don't try to force yourself to be someone you're not—which takes us right back to the question of who you are and how you define success. Some artists actually feel so strongly that risk is integral to what they do and how they grow artistically that they purposefully seek out work that scares them. Kate Winslet for one has been widely quoted as stating that she "wouldn't dream of working on something that didn't make my gut rumble and my heart want to explode."

If you're seriously risk averse, if you hate change, if the thought of doing something you've never done before or appearing in front of a live audience makes you break out in a cold sweat, you might need to rethink what success means for you—maybe it's working at a smaller company, doing community-based work, or taking smaller roles. Maybe that's your brand: you're great at what you do; you're dependable; you show up and give it your all every day. Those of us who administer arts organizations need and depend upon people like you. Or it might even mean that filming or recording in a studio setting or working behind the scenes is the right choice for you. Again, it comes down to determining what it is about performing that is truly meaningful to you and what special gift you have to provide.

Opera in the Digital Age

"Since I began my career, the music industry has undergone radical changes in every genre, classical music included. Digital distribution of recorded music has been slower in its effect on classical, but the general direction is the same. The days of walking into the 'opera room' at Tower Records to thumb through CDs are over. There are advantages to this. Music doesn't have to exist in silos, physically separated by genre. Listeners can follow their musical interests wherever they lead, with the click of a mouse. There has been a vast expansion of available, free ways to encounter the arts and entertainment, and not only via the Internet. Even older programming platforms like television have gone from a handful of networks to thousands of choices. I remember, as a student, constantly spending precious time and energy chasing recordings of music I needed to research. Now a performer can find almost anything on YouTube, or music streaming sites, and often multiple recordings of the same piece.

"However, without the filter provided by the major labels, it can seem overwhelming to peruse the amount of music that's available now. Labels provided a service by screening new talent, promoting potential stars, and coaching them on media engagement."

—Renée Fleming

SUCCESS IS PERSONAL—BUT ALSO RELATIVE

Assuming you're now certain this is your path, it's time to envision the end goal. I know that when I was in the corps of ABT, there were dancers I looked up to as stars, who had achieved what seemed to me like phenomenal levels of success. But when I spoke to them many years later about their careers and told them how much I admired them, I was truly shocked to hear responses like, "Yes, I had a good career, but I was never as good as so-and-so. He (or she) was truly brilliant!" In fact, Kevin McKenzie, formerly a principal dancer of ABT and currently the company's artistic director, is a prime example of how unproductive such comparisons can be. Despite having achieved the highest levels of success in his profession, at the time he was dancing he was also comparing his own career unfavorably to some of his contemporaries. Only in retrospect has he realized that those comparisons were not necessarily helpful or fair, but they were significant to him at the time. Hearing this from Kevin and others has made me realize how subjective (and elusive) a thing success really is, even for the most elite performers.

With that in mind, when it comes to self-assessment, there is also the issue of how you personally define success. Most of us, I'd guess, start out determined, or at least hoping, to become stars—maybe a leading soprano or tenor with an opera company, a principal dancer with a ballet company, concert master in an orchestra, name above the title in a Broadway show. But the fact is that for the vast majority of us, this will not happen, and given the changes in the field, it is even less likely to happen now than it was twenty, thirty, or forty years ago. As a performer in today's world, you may need to recalibrate your sense of what is successful. I know this may sound disheartening, but your ability to embrace and manage its truth could easily determine whether or not you feel fulfilled as a professional.

I know that in the course of my own career as a performer there came a point when I realized I was never going to move beyond being a member of the *corps de ballet*. I was talented, and I worked hard, but there were, quite simply, others who were more naturally gifted than I was, who could do the huge leaps and pirouettes I could never achieve. I came to the painful recognition that there is a level of that indefinable something called natural talent that makes some people stars. The reason they are stars is that they are truly gifted in some special way.

I can still clearly remember standing in the wings of the Metropolitan Opera House watching Gelsey Kirkland perform and realizing that I would never be able to do what she did. I didn't have her natural coordination or stage presence, and no amount of work, rehearsals, or classes was going to change that fact. I needed to accept my limitations and work to make a fulfilling career, even if I was not destined to be the next prima ballerina of American Ballet Theatre.

Even if you are not destined to become the next Baryshnikov, or Yo Yo Ma, or Renée Fleming, or Meryl Streep of your generation, there is still no reason why you shouldn't have an enormously impactful and satisfying career. As an artist, however, you do need to look deeply into yourself and ask what it is you really want from a performing career. If success for you means being a star, and only a star, there are certain choices you will have to make along the way. You may need to ask yourself, "If

I'm not going to be a star, do I quit the field or do I reassess my choices?"

You first need to be clear about what makes the work meaningful to you—the connection with an audience, bringing new life to a classic work, pushing the boundaries of the art form, bringing the performing arts to new audiences in new ways. As Adam Huttler, executive director of Fractured Atlas, a nonprofit organization that supports artists, told me, so long as you are flexible and keep an open mind, there will be many opportunities for you to be successful and feel fulfilled even though your career may end up looking different from what you initially envisioned. But you also need to consider some extremely wise advice I received when I was very young: to be a professional dancer you cannot simply "want it," you must "need it." If you don't "need it," chances are that you will not be truly happy in your career choice. And the same holds true for a career in any of the performing arts.

Remember that the purpose of this book is to help you build a life and a living in the performing arts. Becoming the best you can be as an artist is one key to doing that. The other is finding your own comfort zone within your chosen field. I can't promise you that following my advice is going to make you rich or make you a star, but I can promise that, if you truly need it, I can help you to live a more fulfilling life as an artist while you are also making a living in a field you love.

– Chapter Two –

The Business of Performing Arts

How the Industry Works and How You Can Be a Part of It

There's no business like show business,
but there are several businesses like accounting.

—DAVID LETTERMAN

I suspect that many of you think you already know how the arts industry—or at least your own particular art form—actually works. But it's probably not as simple as it seems—commercial versus not-for-profit companies; freelance contractors versus full-time employees; boards of directors; intellectual property; unions and what they do; agents and managers. These are just some of the "working parts" that fit together to create a business, and if you are to survive and thrive in the increasingly complex, competitive business of the performing arts, the more you know starting out, the better off you'll be. The most wasteful and the saddest outcome I can think of is for an extraordinarily talented artist to give up a career because he or she couldn't figure out

27

how the business works. To me that's not just a loss for the artist but a terrible loss to the arts.

For most of you, it all starts (or started) with your training. Yes, it's true that there are actors and pop singers and band members who "make it in showbiz" without any formal training. But those of you in the classical arts (and many of you who aren't) will probably have spent a good portion of your life in some kind of professional training program. Wherever you are in the process right now, you'll gain something from knowing how various conservatories and professional training schools work, and which ones might work best for you.

WHAT'S THE RIGHT SCHOOL FOR YOU?

As I've already told you, my parents didn't allow me to travel across the country to spend a summer at the Joffrey Ballet School when I was thirteen years old. And as I've also told you, they were right—at least about what was best for me. Every person's circumstance is different, however, and what was right for me may not be right for you. Here are a few important issues you and your parents should be discussing when you're considering your education—in the arts and otherwise.

1. What Is Your Level of Maturity and Your Level of Skill in Your Art?

How prepared are you to leave home and live on your own—for a summer, the school year, or the long-term—at this moment in your life? Will you be living in a dormitory or will you have to find an independent living arrangement? How much support do you (or your parents) feel you need in life and in your art to maximize the chances of your success?

It's always flattering and certainly validating to be accepted into an elite training program, but you have to be ready for it, mentally and emotionally as well as artistically. Some people undoubtedly are ready at a relatively young age, but others might do better being a bigger fish in a smaller pond, receiving more personalized attention, and not having the stress of being so competitive so soon.

I would strongly suggest that before you leave home to enter a major, highly competitive school such as the Juilliard School, the Curtis Institute of Music, the Manhattan School of Music, the Tisch School of the Arts, the New England Conservatory of Music, Berklee College of Music, the Oberlin Conservatory of Music, the Academy of Vocal Arts, the American Conservatory Theater, or the California Institute of the Arts, to name a few, you and your parents look into some of the thousands of summer programs that are available throughout the United States and that, for the most part, have dormitories and cafeterias to accommodate young students. These programs are a wonderful way to gain your introduction to living away from home and learning more about your field of choice. Speak to your local teacher about recommending one or more of these programs, which is what my ballet teacher did for me.

When you do leave home for the entire school year, there is usually someone affiliated with your performing arts school who will help you to organize your living arrangements. Some young students, for example, will live in a group home or apartment overseen by a housemother. At ABT there is one person whose entire job is to take care of student life, and most schools will do whatever they can to help you, if for no other reason than the fact that it is yet one more way to convince you to choose their institution over another.

2. How Certain Are You That You're Ready to Commit?

Any conservatory or professional training institution is demanding, and can even be grueling. If you're certain of the path you want to take, you'll no doubt revel in all that's asked of you, even if you're sometimes exhausted. If you're not sure, the experience will help you to decide one way or the other. As a dancer or a classical musician you will need to make that decision sooner rather than later, and if you decide to go for it, you will have to give it your all. Not unlike training for the Olympics, to be competitive you must be dedicated. I have met many young artists who ultimately decided that they did not want to devote so much of their life to their art form and chose to engage more minimally instead. One young dancer, for example chose to turn down a scholarship with the Joffrey Ballet to attend Sarah Lawrence College, which has a strong dance program. He never let go of his love of dance and has continued to be supportive of the arts throughout his career. You may have heard of him; his name is Rahm Emanuel and he is currently the mayor of Chicago.

The point is that there's really no right or wrong answer except that you need to do what is right for you. Those who love the arts can participate in and support them in many ways: being a professional performer may not be for everyone, but you can always remain engaged with and help change the world through the arts. What you need to do is forge your own path; don't try to live someone else's.

3. Are You Ready for Rejection?

Of course, any arts training program accepts students who the directors believe are going to do well. But not everyone does, and while it is certainly the function of the school to help their students succeed, if you don't live up to your promise or their expectations, if you fall behind, if you seem to be struggling more than is to be expected, there's a good chance you won't be invited back.

There is generally a significant attrition rate during one's teen years, and competition becomes even fiercer at the college or conservatory level. To understand how many begin the climb and how few make it to the top, imagine that you are looking at a large pyramid: There are many, many hopefuls at the bottom (which arts professionals view as the pipeline) and it's a very steep climb to the top. At Juilliard, for instance, there are only twenty-four dance students accepted per class and even fewer who actually graduate. If you imagine the thousands of students who auditioned for each slot, you will understand how competitive the top-level conservatories truly are.

So, if you cannot handle rejection, you should think long and hard before deciding to pursue a career as a performing artist, where there will always be more rejection than acceptance. The inevitability of rejection (which artists at every level experience) is also why you need to define success for yourself. If you truly believe you have something meaningful and important to say through your art, and if you can define success in a way that allows you to engage meaningfully in your work, you will be able to endure just about any amount of negativity. It is your own belief in your work that matters.

4. Do You Have a Backup Plan?

As you know, my own career as a dancer came to an untimely end because of a serious injury, but there are many things that could derail a performer's career, as well as many reasons why a performer might choose to stop performing. No one's future is set in stone, which is why I am so adamant about the need to keep your options open.

Completing your academic education will be the foundation you'll need to build on should your performing career do an abrupt left turn or come to a standstill for any reason. Some arts schools actually integrate academics into their programs, but most do not. Many schools do, however, hold classes after school hours and into the evening. When I was in high school, I took ballet lessons from four until nine o'clock on weekday evenings and all day on Saturday and Sunday.

If you live locally, see how flexible your high school is in terms of scheduling your classes so that you can pursue your academics while training. Some students are homeschooled, and there are also many online programs available. Taking online classes is certainly a viable option, but if you do go that route, look for programs that are rigorous (not just getting you through). Your performing arts school will probably help you to organize your education just as they do your housing arrangements, and, trust me, investing in your academic education *now* will be critical as you move forward in your life.

Interestingly, although I've always been grateful for having the education that allowed me to shift gears when my Plan A was derailed by injury, Sigourney Weaver gave me a different—and equally important—reason for the value of academic success. She feels that she has been successful partially because of luck, but also because she had a good education. She graduated from Stanford with a BA in English literature and believes that her academic background has allowed her to assess the structure and themes of the scripts she is offered and to choose her projects based on their overall quality rather than being seduced by her specific role.

> "The more you educate yourself, the more you bring to the table. Education helps sustain your career by nourishing your work and making it enjoyable. An education serves as the 'roots' going into the earth."
>
> —Sigourney Weaver

ENTERING TODAY'S WORKFORCE

Just like anyone else, once you've completed your education it's time to go to work. Interestingly, the kinds of work or jobs available to the emerging performer are changing in ways that are not so different from the changing job opportunities in the world at large.

Years ago, most people got a job with a company and often stayed with that company until they received the proverbial gold watch (and, hopefully, a pension) when they reached retirement age. Some people chose to leave corporate life once they'd amassed a fair amount of experience in their field to go "out on their own" as freelancers or to open their own small company. And the same was true in the world of the performing arts.

Young performers might graduate from a conservatory or a college program in the arts and join a company—be it dance, opera, or orchestra—where they stayed, moving through the ranks, for years. If they did leave to form their own company it was generally after they'd gained years of experience, and if they appeared as a guest performer it was as an adjunct to their main work with a company.

Now both the arts business and the business world in general are, to large degree, being turned upside down. In the "civilian" world we hear about young people forming start-ups, which, if they succeed, can bring in a lot of money in a very short time.

In the arts business, we're hearing more and more about You-Tube sensations and winners of competitions like *American Idol* or *America's Got Talent* who become overnight sensations. Artists ranging from the very young opera singer Jackie Evancho to the pop idols One Direction were "discovered" (and in the case of One Direction, actually created) on one of these competitions. But, just like those mega-successful start-ups, they are very much the exceptions to the rule.

So why am I telling you all this? Because you need to understand that those of you who will be hired as a permanent member of a company will be the minority, as will those of you who become instantly successful on your own. Most of you will probably be spending a lot of time auditioning, working gigs with limited runs, and being "between jobs." You will, in other words, be working freelance, as opposed to being an employee of a single company. As a freelance worker you will be on your own when it comes to negotiating contracts, paying taxes, and taking care of all your financial obligations. We'll be talking much more about obligations and finances in Chapter 6, but working freelance is also one of the reasons why it's so important for you not only to have a backup plan but also to define your brand and become your own best publicist.

INTELLECTUAL PROPERTY, COPYRIGHT LAW, AND HOW THEY AFFECT YOUR CAREER

Intellectual property is anything over which a person has ownership that isn't "real," in the sense of being a tangible "thing"— from a house to a car to an item of clothing. It might be the words in a book or a play, the tune or lyrics in a song, the notes and arrangement of a piece of music, the design of a costume, or the steps in a dance. Intellectual property is protected by copyright law, which means that it can't be copied, pirated, or simply reused by anyone who chooses to do so.

Acknowledging another person's rights to his or her own intellectual property and protecting your own will be an important aspect of your relationship with the business of the performing arts throughout your career.

With certain exceptions we'll discuss in a minute, if you want to sing a song, perform a dance, stage a play, or play a piece of music created by someone else, you need to get permission from the person who owns the property (or that person's heirs or executors), and, in most instances, pay a fee for the usage. So, for example, if a company wants to mount a Balanchine ballet, that company must get permission and pay a royalty to The George Balanchine Trust, and must work with a Balanchine Trust–approved *répétiteur* to be certain that the ballet is mounted and performed in a way that meets with the trust's approval. When ABT, for example, mounts a production of *Romeo and Juliet* with music by Prokofiev, the company pays a royalty of several thousands of dollars for each performance. When ownership or copyright is in dispute, it can become a legal issue, as it did in 2014 when singer-songwriter Sam Smith's "Stay with Me" seemed to bear a too-distinct resemblance to Tom Petty's "I Won't Back Down." In the end, Smith wound up paying a royalty to Petty.

You may wonder how anyone would know if you used or performed another person's work so long as it wasn't in a well-known or well-attended public arena. But the fact is that there are companies, including lawyers and law firms, whose business it is to watch out for and protect against copyright infringement.

You may have heard about songs, music, books, plays, or other intellectual property being in the public domain. What this means is that the property is no longer protected by copyright law and anyone can use it without permission and free of charge. In fact, one of the reasons early cartoons were set to classical music (think, in particular, *Fantasia*) was that the music was in the public domain. But knowing when something falls into that category can be a bit tricky. For any work created or published after 1977 the copyright lasts for the life of the creator plus seventy years. All works published in the United States before 1923 are in the public domain. But all works published after 1922 and before 1978 (Prokofiev's *Romeo and Juliet* was published in 1936) are under copyright for ninety-five years. So it can get tricky, and if you're in doubt, you'll need to do some research before deciding to use someone else's creation.

Exceptions to the rule include material that falls under the umbrella of fair use, as well as performances for educational purposes—such as those put on at a school (unless the school sells tickets to the performance, in which case they do need to apply for permission) and for the purpose of entering a competition. So, opera singers or musicians, for example, who may enter a number of competitions throughout the year, do not have to worry about copyright infringement. And since school performances do not generally command large audiences or high ticket prices, the fee may be waived when permission is granted. Generally speaking, the fee is on a sliding scale, depending on where, for how long, before how many people, and at what cost the material will be used. Fair use is defined as a small percentage of the total work and will also depend on the reason for which it is used. But that can get dicey, depending on the length of the work as a whole, and can only be determined on an individual basis.

I know it's enough to make your head spin, but it really is something of which any performer or potential creator needs to be aware. At some point you may be starting a small company or mounting a production, in which case you'll have to comply with copyright laws. Or you may be writing music or choreographing a dance, in which case you will certainly want to be sure you protect your own intellectual property rights.

One area in which you may not even think about intellectual property rights—but should—is in terms of photographs. If a photographer takes publicity shots of you, when you negotiate the price you also need to be aware of what you are buying. In most instances, unless you specifically agree otherwise, the photographer will retain ownership of the actual photo, and you will be buying only the right to use it in specific situations. You will need to have a written agreement stating what those rights are, and you will need to be sure you're covering every situation in which you might want to use it; otherwise, you'll have to go back to the photographer to purchase more rights in the future. And you also need to be aware of the fact that if the photographer owns the photo, he can continue to use it in any way he chooses, and you have no control over what he does with it.

Rosalie O'Connor, a professional photographer and a former dancer with American Ballet Theatre, explained to me how important it is to clarify all this with the photographer. For instance, she has seen photos posted on Facebook by people who had not obtained permission and, therefore, did not have the right to use them, and who didn't even credit the photographer for his or her work. As she said, people often think, "It's only Facebook so it shouldn't matter." Well, it does matter. Those photos are "out there" for anyone to see, so you must be sure that you have the right to post them, and you need to give credit where credit is due.

WHAT'S NOT-FOR-PROFIT
AND WHY YOU SHOULD CARE

For many people, the distinction between commercial and not-for-profit is somewhat murky. Many believe that not-for-profit means that a company *cannot* make a profit (or have a budget surplus). This is absolutely wrong. All nonprofits, including those in the arts, can make a profit (and should probably strive to do so). In fact, those that continue to lose money—such as the late, lamented New York City Opera—will eventually have to close.

The true fundamental difference between a commercial entity and a not-for-profit organization is how they use their profits/surplus (if they have any). Legally, if a not-for-profit ends its fiscal year with a surplus, that money must be directed back into the business of the organization. In the commercial world, a company is allowed to choose between reinvesting in its business or distributing the surplus cash to its investors. This is important, because it emphasizes the notion that not-for-profits must be mission based: their goal is to fulfill their mission, which is generally to serve the greater public good, *not* to enrich an investor.

This difference is the reason why not-for-profits accept donations and why the donors get to take a tax deduction. The underlying governmental rationale is that the donations are helping the greater good, and because of that the government has an interest in supporting and encouraging them. In fact, without donations most nonprofits could not continue to exist. Basically, in the nonprofit performing arts world, funds to run the business come both from "earned income," such as ticket sales, tuition fees, and merchandise, and from "contributed income," meaning donations. In a sense, this gives them the ability to pay their artists and create productions that may be risky or groundbreaking, but that cost much more to mount than they could ever earn back from selling seats. ABT, for example, could not turn a profit from ticket sales alone even if it were to sell out the Metropolitan Opera House very single night of the season. This is equally true for the Los Angeles Philharmonic at Walt Disney Concert Hall, the Los Angeles Opera at the Dorothy Chandler Pavilion, the Center Theatre Group at the Mark Taper Forum, or any other similar company and venue.

The ratio between earned and contributed income can vary immensely from one entity to another, but all nonprofits depend on both sources. At ABT, the goal was to have 55 percent of our income earned from ticket sales and tuition and 45 percent contributed by donors. However, for some organizations, such as symphony orchestras, that ratio can be closer to 80 percent donations and 20 percent ticket income.

Because donations are so important, if you work for a non-profit you may be called upon to help raise those funds. At ABT, if we were trying to raise money for a scholarship, we might have the potential donor watch the student in class or performance, and then take them both to lunch or tea so that they can get to know one another. And if we were meeting with someone who could be a really big donor, we might take along one of the company "stars." Similarly, at a recent dance performance at The Music Center, we asked dancers Roberto Bolle and Herman Cornejo to participate in a panel discussion and meet with patrons one-on-one at a cocktail party. In general, if someone feels he or she "knows" the star and is privy to access or information that is not available to the general public, that donor will be more likely to give a more generous amount. There is an old saying in the fund-raising world that "people give to people, not things" and this is very true. Effective fund-raising engages people on a deeply personal and emotional level.

For-profit businesses, on the other hand, are there to enrich their owners as well as their investors, while, hopefully, manufacturing and/or providing a useful product or service to the public. In the theater, for example, that would mean soliciting funds from backers as well as selling tickets. Just as not-for-profits woo donors, producers woo backers by holding special readings or run-throughs, but unlike those who donate funds to nonprofits, the backers of a theater production are hoping to make a profit on their investment (although not so many actually do).

Most, if not all, traditional arts organizations are not-for-profit, which means that if you become a member of a classical dance company, opera, or orchestra, you will be working for a not-for-profit institution. Some of you may think there's something noble about working for a nonprofit, or that it will in some way provide a more congenial or collegial atmosphere. In some sense that may be true; as a member of a mission-based organization, everyone should be focused on striving to help the organization fulfill its mission. But that doesn't mean it is any less rigorous or competitive. Every nonprofit I have worked for is striving for excellence, which means there are high demands placed on the work of everyone involved.

So, not only will the work be as demanding as—if not more than—it would be in a for-profit enterprise, the pay will probably also be less. The point here is that there are always trade-offs, and to be a savvy performer you need to know in advance what those trade-offs are and what kind of situation you are likely to be getting yourself into so that, assuming you are given a choice, you can make an educated decision.

THE ROLE OF THE BOARD OF DIRECTORS

While both for-profit corporations and not-for-profit organizations have boards of directors, the board of a nonprofit has some duties that the board of a for-profit company does not. To begin, it is the board members of the not-for-profit who define the mission of the organization: the reason it exists and what it sets out to accomplish in the broadest of terms, such as, "We aim to bring the highest-quality classical music to underserved communities across America," or, "We aim to bring quality theater education to the children of Dallas, Texas." Once the mission is clear, the board sets out to hire the executives who will help to realize those noble goals. The board of a for-profit business, on the other hand, is primarily tasked with overseeing the activities of the company while also looking after the interests of its owners or shareholders.

Both for profit and nonprofit boards are also legally required to make sure that the organization is being run in a financially sound and responsible manner. Part of that responsibility for a nonprofit board member revolves around helping the organization raise the money needed to ensure that its programs thrive. Most larger nonprofit boards have an expectation of "give or get," meaning that members either have to make a personal contribution to the institution or they have to "get" it from a friend or colleague. Some boards are expected to both "give *and* get." The board establishes these policies, and when you hear about fundraising in an arts organization, you can be pretty sure that the board is somehow involved.

WHY UNIONS MATTER TO YOU

I'm sure that most of you have some idea of what unions do—you know they negotiate members' wages, benefits, and work rules, and you know they have the ability to call a strike if they think it will help their negotiations. As CEO of ABT I negotiated with unions all the time, and even though it is a dance company, there are many different unions involved in day-to-day operations—from dancers' and musicians' to electricians' to stagehands'—just to name a few. As a young dancer, however, I had very little idea of what unions did or didn't do.

I didn't realize that some (in fact most) of the larger companies, including ABT, are unionized and that once I joined the company I would also be obliged to join the union. I didn't know that you could be a member of more than one union (or why I would want to), and I didn't know that I couldn't just march into a union office and sign up if I wanted to. In fact, depending upon the union, joining can be a sort of catch-22 proposition.

The Screen Actors Guild–American Federation of Television and Radio Artists (SAG-AFTRA), for example, represents performers in all three of those media; Actors' Equity represents stage actors; the American Guild of Musical Artists represents ballet dancers and opera singers; and the American Federation of Musicians represents musicians. You have to be hired by a union company, show, or organization before you become eligible (and are, in fact, required) to join the union. So, for example, when I had the opportunity to appear in a couple of commercials—one for Prudential Life Insurance and another for General Electric—I had to join SAG. Part of my union contract stipulated that I would receive a fee (aka residuals) every time the commercials aired, and, as it happened, the one for GE was shown during the Super Bowl and continued to play for years afterward. The residuals I got from that commercial helped me pay my college tuition at Brown.

Obviously, there are both union and nonunion shows and organizations. If you attend an audition, it should be clear if the production or company is union. (If it isn't clear, ask!) If you are hired and you are not a member of the union that has jurisdiction over the production, you will need to join. But joining a union is something to be looked upon as a privilege as much as (or more than) it is as an obligation. For many artists, being hired by a union company or production is just the opportunity they've been waiting for in order to join a union.

Once you are a member, whenever you work in a union production or for a unionized company, you pay a portion of whatever you earn to the union, and in return your terms of employment are determined by a union contract that includes certain protections and benefits. Those protections and benefits do, however, have specific parameters. While a performing arts union cannot, for example, involve itself in artistic matters, such as casting or the stylistic choices of the director, it can offer protections if you are fired. (There may be contractual terms the employer must adhere to, such as notification requirements and severance pay.) And a union will fight for fairness in pay, health-care benefits, safety in the workplace, and the nonexploitation (such as demanding work for no pay, or harassment) of its membership by management.

You should also know that the same union negotiates different deals with different companies, so a particular union's contract with ABT will be different from its contract with the Los Angeles Philharmonic, the Center Theatre Group, the Metropolitan Opera, or even with New York City Ballet. And, in addition, not all unions offer the same benefits. When I did that commercial work and joined SAG years ago, I found that the medical benefits I got from the Screen Actors Guild were better than those offered by my dancer's union. So even though it would mean paying dues to more than one union, it may well be worth your while, not only because of the benefits offered but also because, in some instances, belonging to more than one union might provide you with a wider range of employment opportunities.

AGENTS AND MANAGERS

Unions negotiate terms for companies (or productions) as a whole, not for any single individual. Yes, you can go to the union if you feel that the terms of your employment have been violated in some way, such as not receiving pay for working overtime or finding that your benefits were calculated incorrectly. But there are many things a union cannot and will not do for you as an individual that an agent or manager would do.

Agents and managers (also known as personal representatives) work for individual clients (although, of course, they may have several or many); unions, in effect, work for groups. An agent may put you forward for a particular job and also negotiate the terms of your contract. Unions do not recommend one member over another for a job, and they negotiate contracts for their members as a group, not for individuals.

While both agents and managers work for individual clients,

their roles are actually quite different. An agent finds or receives offers for work and usually negotiates the terms of the contract. Just as some performers work freelance while others are members of a company, there are agents who work on their own and others who are members of large agencies, such as the William Morris Agency, International Creative Management (ICM), Columbia Artists Management Inc. (CAMI), and Creative Artists Agency (CAA), that have many clients in many fields and large staffs to represent artists all over the world.

In contrast to talent agents, who specialize in getting jobs for their clients, managers or personal representatives are usually concerned with the artist's long-term goals and are responsible for day-to-day career management, which includes providing personal advice and overseeing finances. Managers may also serve as buffers to insulate an artist from requests for endorsements, guest appearances, PR opportunities, and other activities not directly related to actual performance. Because of the broader scope of their duties, managers usually have a smaller number of clients. According to Peter Diggins, a longtime performing arts manager, the relationship between an artist and his/her manager is a deeply personal partnership. There must be good chemistry and a sense of trust between the two. If there isn't, it would be in the best interests of both parties to simply move on.

Agents and managers earn their living by getting a percentage of a performer's income—generally 10 to 15 percent for agents (although the rate will depend on the state in which the contract or agreement is negotiated, the particular union involved, and the length of the job the agent has secured for his or her client) and 15–25 percent for managers (whose fees are not regulated). As far as you're concerned, that means two things: first, it's yet another bite out of your paycheck, and second, most agents and managers worth their fees won't take you on until you're already established and earning enough money to make it worth their while, or if they see a significant upside potential for your career and want to sign you before someone else does. Bottom line: they need to sign performers they think can earn them income, not because they are greedy, mercenary beings but because they need to earn a living, just like everyone else. Agents or managers who love the performing arts but cannot find jobs for the artists they represent will not last very long in the business. Therefore, the harsh reality is that they are going to be looking for those artists who they believe have the potential to generate performance fees, not those—no matter how talented and/or cutting-edge they may be—whom no one wants to hire.

Initially, most young performers will be going it on their own, and that's where having a strong personal brand comes into play. Those who will become the most successful are the savviest self-marketers, those who negotiate most successfully, and those who have the clearest idea of what direction they want to take within their particular art.

CONNECTING ALL THE MOVING PARTS

Yes, it's a lot to take in. Yes, the arts business is extremely multifaceted. And that's exactly why it's so important that you go into business with as much information as you can gather in advance. While the particulars may vary from one art form to another, the broader concepts remain the same:

* Whether you're hired by a unionized company directly after school or join one in the future, you need to know what a union can and cannot do for you—and what you must do in order to join one.
* You ought to be aware of the differences—and similarities—between commercial and not-for-profit enterprises, so that you don't have unrealistic or idealistic expectations of either one.
* As a performer, you need to know who owns what in terms of the works you perform, and how to protect your rights to the ones you create.
* You should be aware of what agents and managers do.
* And you must, to whatever extent possible, remain in control of every aspect of your career so that you don't get taken advantage of (as I did early in my career when my agent failed to pass on money he'd collected on my behalf).

REMEMBER: You can't have control until you have knowledge.

Chapter Three

Promoting Brand "You"

Projecting Your Voice and Getting Yourself Heard

It's what you do that makes you who you are and
how you project that to others that makes you memorable.

—DAN SCHWABEL,

**MANAGING PARTNER OF MILLENNIAL BRANDING AND
AUTHOR OF *PROMOTE YOURSELF: THE NEW RULES FOR CAREER SUCCESS***

Now that you've established a foundation as an artist—that is, found your voice and your mission, started to define what success looks like to you, and learned the fundamentals of the industry—the next big piece of the puzzle is how to make yourself known.

In the business world—and remember that the performing arts *is* a business—this is called marketing, or, more recently, branding your product. As a performer, you are the product, so what you are marketing is yourself. Your brand is your image as an artist. What makes you different from others in your field? What do people think of when they hear your name? Why would they come to see you as opposed to some other dancer, singer, actor, or musician? On the most basic level, what makes Bounty different from Scott paper towels? How does Chobani differentiate itself from Fage Greek yogurt? Not everyone is going to prefer you to some other brand, but the more people there are who recognize and choose you, the more likely you are to become a leader in your category.

Connecting Through Branding

"While winning competitions and securing artist management are still important roads to discovery, technological advances have created new ways for performers to connect to audiences outside of institutional structures. To be successful, young artists will need a strong entrepreneurial spirit, and time and creativity to devote to this side of the career. Beyond a singer's talent and technique, which are indispensable, finding a marketing edge; i.e. *what sets one apart* [emphasis added], is now crucial. Mastery of social media, web presence, and cultivation of image are key. With the ever-increasing importance of video, especially in opera, the ability to convey a believable, appealing presence on camera is also becoming a necessity.

"I would suggest taking courses in digital editing and website creation, personal finance, and even general business and marketing. Given the challenging economics, we need to take responsibility for our own career growth, even if we have the benefit of professional management. We have to work together with managers now to strategize, create a digital profile complete with videos and recordings, and leverage social media to engage audiences.

"Learning the business side of the arts is crucial, especially

> now; but without solid technique, and care of the instrument and the artistry, there will be no career, at least not one that will last. Whatever the pressures of the business, and they may be great, attention to the craft and the artistry of performance has to come first."
>
> —Renée Fleming

Although she is talking about setting yourself apart specifically in the operatic world, what Renée Fleming has to say is equally applicable to all the performing arts. I know that all this may sound crass and distasteful to the artist in you. But in the volatile, noisy, dog-eat-dog atmosphere of the current performing arts business, it is necessary, even though it may be (or seem to you) a necessary evil. If you don't think about your image and how you can differentiate yourself in the marketplace, you simply will not be competitive. And if you think that just because you are talented and working as hard as you can, people will naturally find you, you're on the fast track to hiding your light under the proverbial bushel—or, to quote another cliché, flying under the radar.

So let's talk about some of the myths you may have heard about a personal brand.

Myth 1:
Doing great work = having a great reputation.

Not true. In fact, we all know people who have great reputations and are not doing great work. Or, conversely, artists who we know should have been more successful than they were but spent their careers living in the shadows because they could not compellingly project their value or the value of their work.

Myth 2:
The company or my director will market my brand.

While it is true that your director, artistic leader, or the artistic staff may think you are a wonderful artist and may acknowledge as much, you cannot expect them to have the time or the ability to promote you. Until you get to the point where your name is so well known that it draws audiences to your performances, which means that you are already a "big name," you will have to promote yourself—both internally to your superiors within the company and externally to the public to gain recognition. When Misty Copeland realized that ABT was not in a position to promote her as an individual rather than promoting the company as a whole, she decided to hire a publicist/manager, who has worked so well with her that she is now one of the most recognized classical dancers in the world.

You must take responsibility for your own brand and your own career. This means that it's up to you to make your presence known. Don't hide in the back of the class; take your place front and center like that little kid I saw in the video, and if you are lucky enough to attend a reception or event where you have the opportunity to meet people who can advance your career, step up, shake hands, and introduce yourself. (For more on how to do this effectively, see Chapter 4.)

Myth 3:
Self-promotion is boastful and bad.

For an artist, humility is a double-edged sword. Yes, you must recognize that you are here to serve the art form, not the other way around, but being so humble that it appears even you don't believe in yourself is counterproductive. My advice is instead of thinking about what you're doing as "self promotion," you think of it as educating people about your brand, your image, and your special voice. Remember, if you don't believe that you are making a special contribution to the field, you shouldn't expect others to do so, either.

THE POWER OF THE WEB

The need to create and maintain a significant online presence is undoubtedly one of the greatest changes in the world of the performing artist, and it all started less than ten years ago. The World Wide Web itself didn't make its debut as a publicly available service until August 1991, and only fourteen years later, in 2005, YouTube was born. Technology—and, therefore, dissemination of information—is moving faster and faster, and if you're going to get yourself out there, you have to keep up or be left behind.

The good news and the bad news is
virtually anyone on earth can find out almost
anything about you anytime they want.

You have multiple opportunities to inform the public about who you are and what you're doing because the gatekeepers have, in effect, deserted their posts and left the gates wide open. Although, as I've already mentioned, you may, down the line, have an agent and/or a manager to take care of your publicity and promotion, at least in the beginning you must and should be your own best publicist, and you have all the tools you need literally at your fingertips free of charge.

The bad news is that the traditional patron population for the performing arts is aging out, and it's really up to you young performers to attract the next generation. The good news is that these younger people, like you, came of age using social media, and you can now use that familiarity to woo prospective fans and followers.

Daniil Simkin, now a principal dancer with American Ballet Theatre, was among the first ballet dancers I'm aware of to take advantage of the power of social media. When the company was performing in Beijing a few years ago, he stepped into a leading role at the last minute, tweeted out his good fortune to his Twitter followers, and invited any of them who were in town to come to the performance. After that, he continued to keep people electronically informed of what he was doing, and now, during our off-season, he's being offered gigs around the world and is able to command more money because of the international visibility he's been able to develop and maintain. Of course, it should be taken as a given that he is a very talented dancer, but, as I keep saying, you can be extraordinarily talented and it won't mean a thing if no one knows who you are or where to find you.

Two artists who have made phenomenal use of the electronic and social media available to push their careers to new heights are the cellists Luka Šulić, a Slovenian, and Stjepan Hauser, a Croatian, who together form the duo known as 2Cellos. Both classically trained, they were having financial difficulties when a friend suggested that they try breaking into the pop market by making a video of the Michael Jackson song "Smooth Criminal." They did. Then they posted it on YouTube, where they were discovered by Sony Masterworks. Now known for playing covers of well-known pop and rock songs, they've released three albums. They've played with Elton John at the Queen's Diamond Jubilee concert at Buckingham Palace and as part of his world tour, and have appeared on the American television series *Glee*, in a commercial for a Japanese mobile phone company, and in many other international venues. It was initially their savvy use of electronic media, as well as their willingness to try something different from the kind of music they'd been trained to play, that helped to catapult their career to international popularity and acclaim. If you can't get comfortable with change and make it work for you instead of against you, no matter how much you love your chosen field, you may find that you don't love your life as a performer.

As I've said before, a good artist is educated, and the very same online tools used by Daniil Simkin and others for self-promotion are wonderful resources with many applications. Lang Lang, the great classical pianist, also points out how technology has increased the reach of classical music to encompass a younger and broader audience.

"Through the various search engines, an infinite amount of music can now be downloaded from a number of distributors and stored in devices such as MP3s. This great leap in technology has played an incredible role in opening the world of classical music to everyone, particularly to the younger generation.

"The introduction of the YouTube ten years ago now gives us access to visual performances by artists past and present. Music lessons, at every level, of any instrument, may be found. Auditions to competitions may be submitted through YouTube.

"The streaming of concerts and operas worldwide to local theatres has given the opportunity, particularly to young people, to see live performances for a fraction of the cost of attending them in the concert halls.

"We owe much gratitude to the innovators of all these technological advancements for enriching our lives in ways we never dreamed of."

HOW TO BUILD A WEBSITE

One of the most powerful tools the savvy performer can have for marketing his or her brand is a personal website.

No longer a complicated technical process that requires hiring a Web designer and an outlay of what could be several thousand dollars, creating and managing your own website is now relatively "do it yourself'" and straightforward. Here are the basic steps you'll need to follow.

* First, you need to get a domain name. There are numerous services through which you can do this. The name should be something that is directly tied to your name or your brand so that it will be easy for people to

find if they search for you online. Mine, for instance, is rachelsmoore.com.

* Second, choose from among any number of tools, including services like Squarespace or WordPress, to quickly build your own website.

* Third, think about what content you will want to put on your website. You can post photos of yourself, videos, music clips, information on upcoming or past performances, reviews, and a blog. Keep in mind that what you put on your website is public. There are complicated rules about what remains within your copyright or trademark when it hits a website or social media, so be very careful about what you post if you want to maintain its integrity in terms of intellectual property.

* If you decide to blog, remember that you need to add new posts on a regular basis. Otherwise people will stop visiting your site.

* Finally, be sure that your website is linked to all of your social media sites, such as Facebook, Twitter, Instagram, and Pinterest, so that visitors to any of those accounts can access it easily.

MAKING "FRIENDS" ON SOCIAL MEDIA

One significant aspect of the proliferation of social media is that all kinds of people look upon performing artists as people they know. And they are constantly hungry to know more and more. They want to be your friends and your followers; they want to like you. You've just got to reach out and offer them your virtual hand.

It wasn't always that way. While talented people have historically been recognized and appreciated for their talent, their audiences didn't always look upon them as social equals—much less people they would want to have as friends. I was reminded of this change in public perception while watching an episode of *Downton Abbey* in which the great Australian soprano of the Victorian era, Dame Nellie Melba (she of the eponymous Melba toast and peach Melba, played, fittingly enough, by the great New Zealand soprano Kiri Te Kanawa) was invited to Downton to sing in the parlor. While family members and their guests were delighted to hear her, they were not at all pleased with the notion that she (a performer!) would sit down at the dinner table with them. Carson, the butler, was horrified at the thought of having to serve her, and initially she was served separately in a different room, until Lady Cora (who is, incidentally, American) brought her in to join the others. Similarly, ballet dancers and actors were largely shunned by polite society in earlier times, when they were generally believed to be people of loose morals or even criminals.

Now, of course, charities make a lot of money by auctioning off a dinner with some well-known entertainer. Everyone wants to be able to claim an A-list personality as his or her friend, or at least to be able to say they've met socially. Times have definitely changed, which is great for young performers who are building a reputation and a fan base.

The potentially bad news (depending on how tech-literate and proactive you are) is that it's up to you to make the most of all the online wealth that's available for the taking. And you need to stay on top of it—tweeting, posting, Instagramming, and so on—because if you don't keep reminding people that you're out there and want to connect with them, they'll lose interest and start looking for newer, more proactive "friends."

Before you begin, however, there are a few rules you need to learn and follow in order to be sure your use of social media helps to move your career forward and doesn't unintentionally derail it.

1. Be careful what you post. By putting something in writing you are creating a permanent record that can be referred to and shared and reshared forever, with no ability on your part to control or influence it. Post only statements you would feel comfortable sharing with employers, potential employers, patrons, or clients. And, unless it is part of your brand, steer clear of highly controversial topics or overtly sexualized photos or commentary. Don't be mean or gossipy. Take the high road and be gracious.

2. Consider having two accounts: one just for your very close friends and one for business. But be careful: even accounts targeted to close friends can become "public," so watch what you post.

3. Talk about your professional successes, but try to make your posts sound more like an Academy Award acceptance speech than a paid advertisement. Be genuine in your excitement and grateful to those who supported you in your endeavors. Once again, be gracious and compliment others on their successes.

4. Post only photos of yourself that support your brand. Carefully select your profile photo. This is the image people will see most often, so find something that is compelling and attractive. Photos to avoid include wild party pictures or those taken in situations where alcohol or drugs are involved. Untag yourself if you've been tagged in unprofessional or unacceptable photos posted by others. You may not have control over what your friends post, but you can untag yourself so that your own network won't be able to view them. You can also consider asking friends to delete any photo that is particularly embarrassing to you.

On the flip side of that coin, if a professional photographer took your photo, it is important to credit that person. It was his or her work, so, questions of copyright aside, it's just the right thing to do. Imagine how you would feel if you were performing and your name didn't make it into the program. You would probably be very upset. Everyone wants their work to be recognized, but especially as artists, we have an obligation to honor and recognize other artists' creative endeavors.

How Do You Choose Your Head Shots?

How do you present yourself in your head shots? How do you decide what to wear, how to style your hair, how to pose? As you make all those decisions you are, in effect, defining who you are as an artist, and, therefore, creating your brand. You may not think of it that way, but it's true.

Share only those links or friends' information
that will be universally acceptable and not offensive to others.
Unless it is consistent with your brand, do not link to or "like"
highly controversial characters or articles.

When I asked Daniil Simkin for his tips on how to make the most of social media, this is what he told me:

* You must connect on a deep emotional level; tell a story through social media.
* Everything needs to be filtered through how you want to be presented.
* The content must be relatable, visceral.
* Your story has to be strong emotionally, not just rational.
* You want to create a story that is accessible.
* Be generous; expect to give without getting anything back.
* People are not interested in every aspect of you. Some will be interested in your art form, others in, say, your fashion sense.
* There needs to be a balance between giving them what you think they want (what they expect) and something new.
* Social media should not make you sound-self centered.
* People are more interested in your views than in what you do. Make it more personal.

* I work to ensure my social media is in good taste. People will be turned off by social media that is crass or in bad taste.
* Make your posts strategic and thoughtful—part of a plan and an image.

The bottom line: Just give something to the world that adds value to someone's life.

CONNECTING LIVE AND IN PERSON

A big part of being a performer is learning how to engage with your audience. When I talk to performers about public speaking or appearing on television, I can see the look of horror on their faces, so I know that these kinds of interactions can be incredibly scary for someone who has spent his or her entire life in a studio, theater, or rehearsal hall. However, the reality is that, as a performer in the twenty-first century, you will need to engage with the public in a very personal way. And don't worry—up to 75 percent of people have some form of this fear; in fact celebrities Julia Roberts, Bruce Willis, Tiger Woods, and Samuel L. Jackson, to name a few, number themselves among those who have had to overcome it. You can do it, too, and in order to make the most of your opportunities, you'll have to learn to present yourself well.

It is extremely common for performers to be asked to speak to patrons, to help publicize a performance, to talk to the media about an interesting collaboration, or to be part of a panel discussion in front of an audience that is also recorded and uploaded onto websites or YouTube. In addition, you should be thinking about public speaking as a way to generate self-promotion. With that in mind, you might want to seek out speaking engagements in schools, on public access TV, or try videotaping yourself and posting the video on social media.

Here are a few tips for speaking in public, be it to a group of donors, patrons, potential employers, on TV, or to a newspaper or magazine reporter.

* **Be authentic.**

   Don't try to pretend you are something you're not or adopt contrived mannerisms. Yes, you'll need to be on your best behavior, but that doesn't mean "acting." BE YOURSELF!

* **Be honest.**

   Don't exaggerate your background or experience. First of all, that's lying, and second, you'll probably get caught.

   Be passionate about your work.

   If you sound like you don't care, why should anyone else? If you make it clear how much you love what you do, your audience will be more likely to embrace it—or at least be intrigued enough to explore it further.

* **Be polite.**

   People don't like arrogance or meanness, and while we might enjoy hearing a bit of gossip, we don't like gossipers because their next victim could be us.

* **Understand your audience.**

  Is this a group of people who are knowledgeable about the arts, or do you need to educate your audience about your work? Getting it wrong either way can mean disaster. Those who are knowledgeable don't want you to talk down to them, and those who are unfamiliar with your work or your discipline will stop listening if they don't understand what you're talking about, if you use terms they don't understand, or if you throw out names as if they should know who these people are.

* **If you're nervous, don't apologize.**

  By doing so, you simply draw attention to an issue that, had you not mentioned it, most people wouldn't have noticed.

* **Always make sure that what you are saying is consistent with your brand.**

  Academy Award–winning actress Jennifer Lawrence, for example, is someone who has a strong and consistent brand. In every interview she gives, in all her professional interactions, she is known for being smart, humble, thoughtful, and for taking her work as an actor very seriously.

No matter the interaction, these are important tips to keep in mind anytime you connect with others, including while networking, which we'll discuss in depth in the next chapter.

Cross-Promotion

Stars of stage and screen, singers, dancers, and sports icons appear in advertisements and promote products—or put their brand on products developed especially for them. It's a two-way street: their appearances guarantee that their faces will be "out there," and the fact that they've been chosen by a product's manufacturer or a service provider is a testament to their popularity and instant recognizability—which then reflects back on the product itself.

Lang Lang is, without doubt, one of the greatest and most successful classical pianists of our time. He is a combination of extraordinary talent and extraordinary flair, or as journalist Emma Pomfret wrote in the *Sunday Times,* "I can think of no other classical artist who has achieved Lang Lang's broad appeal without dumbing down." He is one of less than a handful of people guaranteed to fill any concert hall, and he also has endorsement deals with Sony, Audi, and Rolex, as well as his own line of tennis shoes. His name appears in the social pages almost as often as it does on the music pages. But the foundation for all his success is unequivocally his talent.

Lang Lang's artistry is marked by precision, elegance, and drama—qualities that the companies with which he partners also look upon as theirs. By clearly establishing *your* brand, you make yourself recognizable for a specific set of principles and strengths, and you are positioning yourself to collaborate with groups that stand for and operate on the same foundations.

With so many possibilities out there, so much to think about, and so many ways to both help and potentially hurt your career, you're going to need assistance along the way. Just remember to always keep your brand in mind as you build your platform and share your voice. In the following chapter we'll be talking about the kinds of people you should be seeking to join your team, and where you might find them.

Chapter Four

Who Can Help?

Establishing a Network of Support to Guide the Way

Sometimes, idealistic people are put off the whole business
of networking as something tainted by flattery and the pursuit of selfish
advantage. But virtue in obscurity is rewarded only in Heaven.
To succeed in this world you have to be known to people.

—SUPREME COURT JUSTICE SONIA SOTOMAYOR

Having read the first three chapters you now have a pretty good idea of who you are as a person and a performer, how to start defining your brand, and how important it is to make yourself heard. But when it comes to getting your message out there, you may still be wondering where to start.

I've already talked about the executive recruiter who wisely counseled me to take jobs that would help me fill the gaps in my résumé in order to make myself competitive when seeking a position in arts management.

Another equally important and insightful piece of advice came from a friend at the point when I was thinking about going to law school. My friend, who at the time was the executive director of Volunteer Lawyers for the Arts and who knows me very well, suggested that I'd probably be more fulfilled doing something in arts management that would improve many artists' lives on a daily basis than I would sitting in an office writing legal briefs or appearing in a courtroom defending individual artists' First Amendment rights.

They were both right, and luckily I followed their advice. To this day, I believe that I'm doing the work I do because those two people gave me the right advice at the right time and I was willing to listen to what they had to say. We all need the advice and support of people we trust in order to move forward personally and professionally. But we also need to be open to what they're saying and willing to act on it. Think, for example, of where those two young cellists' careers might be today if, instead of listening to the friend who suggested they try the pop music market, they had said, "Don't be ridiculous; we're classical cellists; we don't do that stuff!"

With so much to do and learn, it's essential to tap into the intelligence of others. No one succeeds on his or her own. We all stand on the shoulders of those who helped us at critical times with advice, wisdom, or just plain common sense.

Whether they're your peers, older and wiser professionals, teachers and coaches, accountants and attorneys, managers, agents, or trusted friends and family, you're going to need a network of helpers to get ahead. You'll need to develop connections and cultivate contacts with people who can objectively critique, guide, and nurture you artistically as well as pass along practical tips about the business of performing and the business of life. To do all that, I should add, you will also need to give back. If you want others to help you, you have to be willing to share. Networking is interactive; it's not a one-way street.

FINDING YOUR FELLOW TRAVELERS

If you're just starting out, the connections you make with others who are also at the beginning of their careers may well become some of the most treasured and enduring relationships in your life. In addition, you will discover that many people who are farther along the path remember what starting out was like and are willing to lend a helping hand. When I spoke with Adam Gwon, a writer for musical theater who attended the Tisch School of the Arts at New York University, he mentioned how amazed he is that the people he went to school with have remained active participants in his professional network. It's a sentiment that was echoed by Siobhan Burke, a modern dancer and dance writer who told me that her professional network really started when she was in college and that she continues to work with these same people ten years later.

If you've already embarked on your career, you probably know that it helps immeasurably to have company on the journey, not just to commiserate with but also to bring a different perspective to your work. In fact, the broader, deeper, and more varied your network is, the broader, deeper, and more varied your career is likely to be.

Seeking that kind of connectivity may not come naturally to you, especially if you were trained to be a soloist from the time you were old enough to hold a bow or point a toe. But unless you're that incredibly rare child prodigy, most of you are going to at least start out as members of some kind of group. It can never hurt to have a check in that box on your report card that says "plays well with others."

There's no harm in wanting to be a soloist, or even a star. But having a soloist *attitude* can hamper the growth of your career. Even the greatest performers wisely seek out people they know and trust, from coaches who listen, encourage, and assist, to managers who advise, arrange, and negotiate.

If your solo mindset comes from a feeling that purposefully setting out to seek contacts is somehow inauthentic, rest assured that you don't have to be a slick talker in order to be a great networker. Just the opposite. In networking, insincerity can be spotted a mile away.

Finally, if you think that asking for help will be seen as a sign of weakness, I can assure you that, looking back on those times in my career when I didn't do as well as I could have, I see that one reason was always my fear of asking for help. I wish now that, when I was still dancing, I had asked the ballet masters and mistresses for regular feedback. It would have been incredibly helpful to know what they thought were my strengths and weaknesses and to ask them how I could correct those areas where I needed to improve. Asking for information, advice, or feedback from others actually shows self-awareness and a sense of security.

What Makes a Good Network?

* **A good network is fluid.** It grows and changes as you do. It not only reflects who you are right now in your career but also helps to shape you professionally and maybe even personally.

* **A good network has multiple levels.** You may be very close to and in frequent contact with some people, such as teachers, classmates, roommates, and work colleagues. You may be in touch with others less often, but your connection with those more distant folks may be important or helpful in specific ways at particular times—for example, a videographer, website designer, or that friend of a friend who tells you where to buy affordable, superdurable-but-lightweight luggage to take on tour.

* **A good network knows things you don't.** Your network should help you keep pace with your industry. It should be a place where you both acquire and share information and success strategies. I remember speaking with one young performer who said with great conviction that a particular performing arts company she knew of didn't promote from within. I suggested that this probably wasn't entirely true and shared my perspective on the issue, which was that, at least in major dance companies, the decision to promote someone to principal had to involve asking the question: "Can this person fill four thousand seats?" I'm sure this was something that young performer had not previously considered, but gaining that insight into the business side of the arts would help her to communicate and negotiate more effectively with decision makers in the future.

* **A good network can be a launching pad for new ventures.** Some people in your network may become your creative business partners—perhaps composing, choreographing, writing new works, or forming an ensemble.

* **A good network helps you navigate change.** We've already discussed the fact that, more and more, performers need to adapt quickly to changing conditions. Jobs begin and end; performing companies, businesses, and shows open and close; marketing strategies and technologies change; public tastes fluctuate. A good network vibrates with breaking news and should include people who know how to embrace change. Those whom you probably should avoid including in your network are the people who complain, whine, reject, or otherwise crawl under a "Rock of Resistance"—unless, of course, you can help *them* to change!

* **A good network keeps you company.** No artist is an island. Trying to develop as an artist and make a career of it is hard work. You need to surround yourself with a group of fellow adventurers in the arts who understand the ups and the downs because they're living them, too.

YOUR PERSONAL BOARD OF DIRECTORS

I believe it's important to gather a group of very special people to be your closest advisors. I like to think of them as your personal board of directors.

Businesses build boards composed of people with diverse skill sets to help them achieve a variety of goals. On The Music Center's board, for example, there are financial specialists, legal experts, individuals with marketing and public relations backgrounds, people connected with media and political networks, and education experts. Their varied perspectives help us build strategies that are comprehensive and well thought out in order to become a stronger, more adaptive, more productive business. Yours should help you do the same.

At one time, when people often spent an entire career rising through the ranks at one company, professionals tended to lean on a single mentor to act as their guide. If you have one such person, whether you find one or are one, consider it a tremendous gift. But in the current business climate, the one-mentor model may also be limiting. For one thing, artists as well as people in general tend not to stay in the same workplace very long, which makes it difficult to maintain that long-term connection. Your mentor might leave the company or a new director might come in and have a very different view of the artistic product or performance. When Peter Gelb replaced Joseph Volpe as general manager of the Metropolitan Opera, for instance, he had his own opinion of which artists he wanted to market, and how to expand opera audiences. In such a situation, you don't want to be viewed as clinging to ideas or methods that are now seen as belonging to the past. Being flexible and adjusting to a changing work environment will be a lot easier if you have a more diverse group of advisors, including those who are going through the same changes you are and who may already have survived one or more changes in management.

In addition, the performing arts business has become so complex that one person rarely possesses all the skills necessary to help a protégé succeed, which is yet another reason why it's smart to build a small network of people who can assist you on multiple fronts.

Think of your board members as people who have the skills you lack, who help you learn new skills, push or challenge you in different ways, teach by example, tell you the truth no matter what, and understand your professional aims while bringing different points of view to the party. Below are some examples of the types of people you should have on your board.

Keep an open mind. You may know several people who could fill one of these roles, or you may add more categories, based on your particular needs. What follows are simply guidelines to get you thinking and, I hope, excited about who might be on your artistic dream team.

The Connector/Influencer

Connectors are influential professionals who know people in your industry and can help you broaden your network. Examples might include managers, agents, casting directors, production executives, or teachers; established pros who like your work and don't see you as competition—but really, a connector can be anyone who helps you make contact with others. He or she might introduce you to people you should get to know. Or take you as a guest to professional gatherings. Or get you a ticket to a gala performance where you could meet influential people in the business. Or tell you which industry groups are best to join. Or nominate you for membership in those groups.

A connector probably enjoys being around people and can give you the confidence to put yourself forward even if your personal style is not quite so assertive. There are also what I call "quiet connectors"—people with many years of contacts and "street cred" who may not speak up often, but when they do, others listen.

The Expert in Your Field

Perhaps most similar to a traditional mentor, this is someone well respected in your field who can help you develop your talent. It might be a current coach or teacher, or it could be someone you've worked with in the past, who knows your abilities and temperament very well, understands your goals, and has kept up with your development and with the field. He or she should be someone you can confide in about your work, with whom you can be totally candid, and from whom you can expect 100 percent honest feedback—even when it's not easy to hear. If, for example, your goal is to be a solo pianist or a principal dancer and your expert has reason to believe that's not going to be happening for you, he or she needs to tell you that and you need to trust him enough to take his words to heart.

However, your expert can also help you develop something I believe all artists need: an aesthetic value system—that is, a code of ideas and practices that governs your artistic choices. Having an aesthetic value system is different from being an artistic snob. It's really about finding that "voice" we've been discussing and creating a cohesive perspective that reflects who you are as an artist, and therefore is consistent with your brand. Your expert should, therefore, be someone whose artistic tastes are similar to yours, who can challenge your ideas in intelligent ways, suggest new directions, and be a trusted sounding board when you're making career decisions.

The Counselor

A counselor is someone with strong people skills who knows how to listen, and who can help you manage or improve your ability to form business relationships. There's a popular misconception among younger artists that as long as they're "the best" at their craft, they'll get the job. But, for better or worse, it's often the relationships you form—that is, the people you know—that get you in the door and give you access to the decision makers.

Your counselor needs to be someone whose shoulder you're not afraid to cry on when things aren't going well, who will buck you up when you're down, who will set you straight when you're out of line, and who will help you navigate the ebb and flow of your life as a performing artist. Unlike the connector, your counselor need not be a mover and shaker in your business. He or she may not be the one who actually introduces you to the people you need or want to meet. Rather, he or she needs to be wise about life and people, emotionally intelligent, and able to offer insights that will help you to become a better "people person" and get you back on track when you hit speed bumps along the way.

The Strategist (aka Political Animal)

"Your promo materials could really use a face-lift. Everything is looking a little outdated, and when was that photo taken, anyway?" "Okay, so you can't afford to rent an auditorium. How about holding the concert at your church and turning it into a fundraiser for their shelter program?" "Sounds like the ingénue roles aren't coming your way anymore. What about character roles?" "If you want to get a mortgage, the first step is to pay down your debt and stop bouncing checks." "Did you really think you'd get that gig, considering that the person they hired is dating the director?"

A strategist knows how the performing arts business works, is savvy about the unwritten rules, understands interpersonal politics, and tells you the naked truth about it all. This is a brass-tacks person who can tell you frankly about the lay of the land, spot patterns (including self-defeating ones) you might not see or want to admit, help you strategize your career moves, and perhaps even hold you accountable for achieving your goals. Your strategist hears you talk about your dreams and says not, "If you can dream it, it will happen," but rather "What do you need to do to get there?" Does it mean networking with people in a different part of the industry? Building a website or updating the one you've got? Committing to X number of auditions per month? Learning a new skill, style, or type of art form?

Since I'm an idealist, sometimes I need a bit of a kick in the pants to remind me that not everyone operates with the best of intentions or that it's time to update certain aspects of my or the company's marketing materials. While the unvarnished truth isn't always fun for me to hear, it prevents me from being blindsided by unseen obstacles so that I stand a better chance of achieving my goals. It's very helpful for a CEO to have someone like that on their board, because it's all too easy to get surrounded by "yes people." Since you are, in effect, the CEO of your own life as a performer, the same is true for you. We all need strategists to tell it like it is.

The strategist is all about implementation and results. Dare to dream big with your expert and your counselor. Get it done with your strategist.

CHANGE IT UP

As your career develops and your goals and needs evolve, so will the people on your board of directors—particularly those I call your nuts-and-bolts helpers.

These people have specific skills that are critical not only to your professional success but also to your well-being. Think accountant, attorney, financial advisor, bookkeeper, photographer, videographer, recording technician, computer geek and/or website designer, PR consultant. Even health professionals. All your board members can change over time, but these nuts-and-bolts folks may shift more often than others, depending on what's happening in your career and your life. You may not need an attorney until you have to sign a contract or protect your intellectual property. You may not need a bookkeeper until you start your own small performing company. You may not need a physical therapist until you're rehabbing an injury. But at some point you will need them, and that's when the knowledge that your connectors, experts, and strategists possess can be incredibly helpful.

BUILDING YOUR BROADER NETWORK

Once you understand the value of networking, you might feel the need to just plunge in and start passing out business cards to pretty much anyone you meet. But that's really not the best way to go about it, and for several reasons. First, you don't want people to think you're getting to know them only because they might be helpful to your career. Second, it quickly becomes overwhelming and discouraging to think that you have to make every interaction count for something, and if you don't come out of it with a useful lead, you've failed. Who wants to live and work that way (and who wants to be around someone who does)? Third, scattershot networking is inefficient. Yes, it's possible you might make a good business contact in the checkout line at the supermarket. Those kinds of serendipitous surprises are the reason you should always carry business cards in your pocket, bag, or backpack. But you should be striking up impromptu conversations because you want to, not because you're angling for something, and if a good contact comes from it, consider it a nice bonus.

Your networking strategy should be a blend of spontaneity and coincidence coupled with a relaxed but intelligent intentionality. Here are two places to start—and you can return to these points each time you're ready to take your networking game to the next level:

1. Look at the self-assessment you completed in Chapter 1. What professional goals did you identify? How have you defined success, your abilities, and those skills you need to improve? Based on these insights, what sorts of people should you be trying to meet? Where do you want to be in five years?

2. Now ask yourself: Given where I want to be in five years, what do I need to do in order to get there? Your answers will help you figure out your path. It is one thing to know where you want to be; it's another to develop a step-by-step plan for getting there.

Here are some of the people who might help you:

* **Your peers.** They're similar to you in age, training, and aspirations. You *get* each other. You can commiserate about the ups and downs of your developing careers, puzzle over the logistics of living the performing life, share industry news, and trade tips on where to find work, housing, roommates, teachers/coaches, and everything else, from great cheap restaurants to great affordable head shots. They can become dear lifelong professional friends and may become your partners in collaborative ventures down the road. As CEO of ABT I worked with many of the people I danced with professionally, meaning that we had a long-lived, deeply held trust of one another. These are not only the people with whom I danced but also those who helped me decide which teachers to seek out, how to get the best "deal" on dance clothing or shoes, which jobs were worthwhile, and which were going to be a nightmare!

* **Fellow professionals a level or two above you.** They remember what it was like to be in your shoes and know what kinds of information would be helpful to you. They're likely to hear about available work through their grapevine before it goes public. As active players still trying to advance professionally, they're interested in keeping up with changes in the business and trying out new ways to get work or to market themselves. These are people you can learn from and with.

* **People who are doing what you aspire to do.** These are generally seasoned performers. They can explain how the world you want to enter operates, how they pursue work, where the work is, who the players are, and the benefits and drawbacks of doing what you aspire to do. These are priceless connections who, if you're lucky, could become members of your personal board of directors. Almost on a weekly basis, I am now approached by young arts managers asking for my advice. I try to be helpful, if I can, given my time constraints and schedule. And I find that most professionals whose advice you value, do the same. So reach out; the worst that can happen is that the person will say he or she cannot help you at this time.

* **People who are hiring people like you.** Although you may not cross paths with these people on a daily basis, being on their radar even occasionally is an important networking goal. It never hurts to go into an interview, audition, or meeting being able to say to one of the decision makers, "We met at the XYZ benefit last year. It's good to see you again."

* **People in other branches of the performing arts.** By that I mean, if you're a clarinetist, network not only with other clarinetists, other musicians, and people in the music business, but with arts professionals in general. Performance is a collaborative enterprise. A single production may require staging, lighting, scenery, props, musicians, singers, actors, dancers, costumes, a conductor, audiovisual and electronic equipment—

and maybe even an animal or two. Think of those who make all that happen, not to mention those who cast, direct, market, and fund the production. Think of the deep reserves of knowledge and expertise to be found in these individuals—opportunities they might know about based on work they're doing or tips from people they know. Why wouldn't you want to get to know all sorts of talented folks?

One of the best experiences I had when I was a dancer was working as an assistant to the stage manager on a show called *The Golden Land* at the Second Avenue Theatre in New York. My roommate, who was a stage manager at ABT, got me the work so that I could augment my income during one of our layoff periods. I had a blast! I also learned an enormous amount about being on the production side of a performance and about the similarities and differences between live theater and live dance performances. The relationships I formed and the knowledge I gained at that time were invaluable then and have continued to be so throughout my career.

Try to meet those who are knowledgeable in areas you aren't, from whom you might be able to adapt ideas, learn new practices, technologies, marketing methods, and mindsets—and share yours, too. Market research we did at ABT indicated that the people most likely to attend a dance performance (other than dance enthusiasts, of course) are operagoers, followed by music lovers, and that people in the visual arts prefer dance to music, because dance is a visual medium. All of this tells me that there are more points where these disciplines inter-sect than anyone might expect. So go broad, go deep in your networking, and give your career the opportunity to reflect the richness of all the abilities out there.

Networking and Competing: Can They Coexist?

You will probably be networking with people who are also competing with you for work. While performers may travel the world to practice their art, in many ways it's a small community where cutthroats and backstabbers quickly become known. Distance yourself mentally and physically from these people. Find and learn from those who know how to cooperate as well as compete. Good sportsmanship in the performing arts means accepting the fact that when someone gets a particular job there are others who don't. It's that person's good day. Yours will come. Say congratulations and mean it. Be a supportive pro and whatever others are doing right to get the work will rub off on you in the form of mutual goodwill and shared wisdom.

WHERE TO NETWORK

Where should you go to network? Lots of places. Eventually your network itself will start leading you to new people through formal introductions, work referrals, and "You've got to meet so-and-so. Here's his contact info." You'll still be networking, but over time how to do it and with whom will become clearer. Here are some ideas to get you started.

* **Alumni/ae groups.** Sharing an alma mater gives you common ground on which to start a conversation and establish a connection—even if you didn't know each other when you were there. Highly successful alums can be quite receptive to younger alums asking respectfully for a few minutes of their time or a few words of wisdom. If you graduated from a performing arts school, the networking possibilities are even greater, given your common focus.

* **Classes/training.** Most working performers continue to study with teachers, privately or in groups. They also may take classes outside their area of expertise to round out their training and become more marketable: a classically trained actor might study improv and experimental theater; a singer might study dance to get through the dance call in musical theater auditions.

   Working side by side in a class week after week can create a wonderful network of allies. If you study privately, your teacher could be a resource for people and organizations you should get to know.

* **Performing gigs and other jobs.** If you've got performing work, those long hours of rehearsal are good for more than just polishing the performance. Make friends with your fellow performers and with others on the team. And if you have a "day job" to support yourself, you may be able to network there, too. While it's a cliché that struggling artists wait tables, it's true that you may find some good contacts among your fellow servers. In addition, if you're temping, working in an

office, or doing any other kind of job to pay the bills while you audition, you may have colleagues who are involved in the performing arts, know others who are, or who bring specific abilities to the table (those nuts-and-bolts helpers I mentioned above). Or maybe one of your coworkers is planning a wedding or a special party and needs a singer or a musician to perform at the event.

* **Professional organizations.** Professional organizations generally provide a membership directory, offer online discussion groups, and sponsor programs where members can get to know one another.

  I find that the more time I devote to the organizations I belong to, the more rewarding membership becomes. The more programs you attend, the more members you'll meet. Or take it a step further and get involved in the process. Volunteer at events, join a committee, or suggest a new initiative and step up to lead it. If you've been a member for a while, consider serving on the board or holding an office. Being in charge of something—even if it's just setting up chairs for the meeting or signing in the attendees—confers visibility, indicates that you are a reliable person worth getting to know, and offers built-in reasons to meet people. This is especially useful if you're not someone who is naturally outgoing.

* **Workshops, conferences, seminars, and conventions.** Workshops on self-marketing techniques for performers (audition smarts, "meet-the-agent" seminars, head shot how-tos) can be great places to get to know others

in the job hunt trenches. While larger conferences and conventions can be expensive and very busy, with audience members and speakers hurrying from one session to the next, you can make arrangements in advance to meet with specific people while you're there, or simply go to learn, soak up the vibe, and maybe make some new contacts. At sessions, you may connect with fellow audience members and you may also be able to introduce yourself to industry players who are there as guest speakers. Just remember that you will have no more than a minute or two after a session to shake hands, say your name and what you do, tell the speaker how much you appreciate his/her work, and perhaps ask a question. I call this having your "elevator speech"—that is, a well-crafted, short, extremely compelling speech about what you do—ready to go. If you're not sure how to do this, go back and look at the personal tagline you created for yourself in Chapter 1. This will be your chance to make what you learned when articulating to yourself "why" you do what you do understandable and interesting to others. It shouldn't take you any longer than it would to arrive at your floor in an elevator. If you drag things out, you'll just be remembered as that annoying person who didn't know when to shut up.

* **Networking groups and performing artist meet-ups.** Type "networking groups nyc" into your browser, as I just did, and you'll get about 8.8 million results. In networking groups there's no awkwardness involved in asking direct questions about work issues and exchanging

business cards. It's what you're there to do. Meet-ups are another way to get to know like-minded peers. On Meetup.com, a website that lets you find a vast network of local groups with interests of all kinds, a search for "Performing Arts within 5 miles of New York, NY" turned up more than two hundred listings with intriguing names like Technology/Performance Experiments in Tribeca, the NY Musicians Group, and Improve with Improv—Workshops for Actors. Browse the site for a group in your area that is relevant to your interests and goals. (And if you don't find one, why not start one?)

* **Online.** While there's no substitute for the power of in-person networking, industry discussion boards, blogs, and websites can help you learn more about the business and offer the potential to find and connect online with professionals all over the world—which isn't a bad thing when you consider how often performers travel to where the work is. And, as we've already discussed, having your own website and online social media presence is an effective way to develop your own following.

* **Industry organizations may also have vital online communities.** Professional networking sites such as LinkedIn can be great resources for finding people in particular industries or locations as well as reconnecting with people with whom you've worked or gone to school. Remember to check online for alumni/ae groups. On LinkedIn, for example, you can search a college alumnae page for people working in specific geographic locations, businesses, and professions.

Here again, what you get out of these efforts is a function of what you put in. Be gracious, generous, and positive in your online comments, posts, and inquiries. Offer praise, help, ideas, and insights. Ask your questions respectfully and thank people for their help.

HOW TO BE NETWORK-WORTHY

The best networkers know it isn't just about what your network can do for you; it's also about being the kind of person others want to connect with and help. That entails being a good connector and helper yourself, displaying a generosity of spirit that makes you memorable, builds goodwill, and fosters the desire to reciprocate. Here are some best practices in the art of the reach-out:

* **Face-to-Face.** In-person meetings are most effective because we give and receive the most accurate impressions through the total human package, comprising words, vocal tone, facial expressions, and body language.

   After introducing yourself, what do you say? Avoid questions that have yes-or-no answers. That's the surest way to end a conversation before it's even begun. Instead, ask open-ended questions that invite people to elaborate, describe, offer their opinion, or tell you not just "what" but "why." And don't interrupt when they answer. Give the other person a chance to talk. This is not an inquisition. And if you're asked a question, use it as an opportunity to let the questioner get to know you a bit better.

For example:

YOUR QUESTION: How do you know our host?

ANSWER: We went to XYZ music school together.

YOUR QUESTION: That's a great school. I'd love to hear more about the program you were in.

Or:

YOUR QUESTION: What did you think of the performance?

ANSWER: I liked the beginning, but it sort of fell apart toward the end.

YOUR QUESTION: Really! I sort of felt that way, too, but I couldn't put my finger on why. What do you think went wrong?

Or at a networking event:

YOU: Hi, I'm Amanda Jones. I'm a clarinetist Even though I'm classically trained, I also play a lot of jazz and I'm trying to do more of that on a professional level.

THEM: Nice to meet you, Amanda. I'm Abby Farley. I'm a singer—mostly musical theater.

YOU: That's great. I'd love to hear about some of the productions you've been in.

Your goal for this first meeting is *not* to hustle for work, ask a favor, or get the other person to do anything for you. You just want to find some common ground— a shared professional or personal interest, experience, or point of view—or make a positive connection. That shouldn't take long, and it shouldn't make either one of you feel awkward or defensive.

When there's a lull in the conversation and you sense it's time to move on, offer a clear and gracious exit line, a handshake, and a smile: "I've really enjoyed talking with you. Great to have met you!"

Wondering how to do the business card exchange? One easy way is by offering to send the person something related to your conversation: "I just read a review of that show . . . there's an incredible video of that online . . . I've been using this amazing free app . . . I can send it to you—do you have a card?" Then, in turn, offer yours.

Or ask directly: "I've really enjoyed talking with you. Do you have a card, by any chance? Great. And here's mine." Or, if they're not carrying any cards, take out two of yours, write their contact information on one, and give them the other.

Later, you can follow up by phone or email to say thanks, great to meet you, and (if you want and it seems appropriate) to ask about getting together again. You might suggest meeting for coffee or lunch or attending an industry event or performance together. Or, if you've established a mutual interest outside of your professional life, such as running or tennis or going to museums, you could invite the other person to join you. If there's a cost involved, it would be a good idea to make it clear that you'll each be paying your own way—assuming that's your intention.

∗ **Email.** If you're making your first contact with someone by email, you want to avoid being instantly deleted as junk mail or spam because the recipient doesn't recognize your name. So if someone has suggested you contact this person, say so in your subject line: "Contacting you at Jane Smith's suggestion," "Greetings from a friend of Jane Smith," or some variant of that. And say something similar in the opening line of the email to reinforce the mutual connection. Sometimes Jane Smith will even make the introduction by sending an email to the two of you suggesting that you connect.

If you've already met the person and are emailing to follow up, your subject line should be a reminder of how you met (don't assume the other person will recognize your email address or even remember your name): "Great meeting you at the XYZ benefit." Or it might be "Following up as promised" (if that's what you promised to do), or include a reference to something you promised to send: "*Eugene Onegin* video as promised." If some time has passed since your initial meeting, it would be a good idea to put a reminder in your subject line, such as, "We met at Jane Smith's Halloween party."

The level of formality in your subject line and the email itself will depend upon whether the recipient is a peer ("Great meeting you!") or someone who outranks you professionally ("Thank you for taking the time to speak with me" or "So nice to have met you").

In the body of your email, indicate that you really listened and appreciated meeting this person by mentioning something you found memorable about your conversation: "I was so interested to hear your opinion about . . . I hadn't thought about it that way before . . ." or "I really enjoyed our conversation about . . ." or "I was so impressed by your . . ."

If you're not sure what kind of follow-up meeting to suggest, are not yet ready to take that step, or are not sure how receptive the other person would be, just say how much you enjoyed meeting him or her and that "it would be nice if we could get together sometime to learn more about each other's work." If you get a reply saying "yes, let's," you've got the opening you need. If you don't, you can always get in touch again at a later date: "Hi, _____. We met at the XYZ benefit and I really enjoyed our conversation. I was wondering if you might like to meet for coffee and catch up."

* **Phone Calls.** Because so many people screen their calls and may well not pick up if they don't recognize your number or your name on their caller ID, it would be a good idea to rehearse your voice mail message in advance. Keep it short and friendly, but respectful: "Hi Abby, it's Amanda Jones. We met at Jane Smith's Halloween party. I enjoyed our conversation about _____ and was wondering if you'd like to meet for coffee or to see that photography exhibit we were talking about. My number is _____. Looking forward to hearing from you. Thanks!" In fact, it's a good idea to know what you're going to say even if the other person does pick up the phone. It's easy to get flustered in the moment and,

therefore, not put things exactly the way you would have liked.

* **Letters.** Perhaps you remember them—those communications in which words are carefully composed, written by hand on a sheet of notepaper or typed on letterhead, then folded, inserted in an envelope, addressed and stamped, and mailed to a recipient. Because letters are increasingly rare, they definitely get attention. You might send a formal typed letter to a person in a superior position with whom you're hoping to establish a connection or when you're making a special request of someone. Or send a handwritten thank-you note to someone who has gone out of their way to be helpful. And it should go without saying that if someone has agreed to meet with you in his or her office, or if you've been on a job interview, you should follow up with a thank-you note. Believe me, it will be noticed—as will your failure to do so.

MAINTAINING YOUR NETWORK

Once you've devoted a substantial amount of time and energy to establishing your network, you'll want to make sure you maintain it. Keep your contact lists up to date with the information from those business cards you worked so hard to gather. Include notes on how you met the person; the names of his or her spouse, children, or pets; and things you have in common (same teachers; similar training; a shared passion for Stravinsky, chocolate truffles, basketball, or black Labradors). Think how nice it will feel for someone to receive an email from you that closes with: "Please give my regards to Barbara—and I hope Sneakers hasn't been chewing on any of yours lately!" A simple, honest display of personal caring can reestablish a rapport after months or even years of being out of contact.

That said, the best way to keep your network vibrant is not to lose touch in the first place. That doesn't mean keeping in constant contact, which could be annoying or even a bit weird. All it takes is an email or a call now and then to say "Hi, how are you," and catch up. Better yet, send a website link, video, or article you think the person would like. Best of all, send work leads or referrals you think might be of interest. A serendipitous benefit of this would be if the other person happened know about a gig or a job that might be a good fit for you. The simple coincidence of your having popped into their life at that moment could lead to a referral. But don't expect to receive an immediate benefit every time you check in. Do it because it's nice and right, without asking for anything in return. Then, when you really do need some information, advice, a favor, an introduction, or a recommendation, those with whom you've kept in touch will be that much more likely to help you out.

A FINAL WORD: BECOME PEOPLE-SMART

Not long ago I learned about a team-building exercise that started with the participants' completing of a questionnaire designed to help them understand themselves better. Based on their answers, they then examined their behavior when dealing with stress.

Think about how you and those you know deal with stress, frustrations, and failure: these sorts of exercises can teach us a lot about human nature, and the more you know about what makes you and other people tick, the more attuned and sensitive to others you'll be—and the better you'll become at networking.

In all relationships, both participants have to want to "play," so to speak. Networking is no different. Being able to correctly read another person's signals of reluctance will free both of you to move on. In networking, having people-sense means that you don't take it personally when you simply don't connect. There could be many reasons that have nothing to do with you, including that the other person has other things on his or her mind, doesn't want to network at that moment, isn't a good professional match for you, or just isn't very good at networking.

Treat yourself to some good books on human behavior. Two that I like are Howard Gardner's *Multiple Intelligences: New Horizons in Theory and Practice,* and Daniel Goleman's *Emotional Intelligence*. Watch how the people-smart people you know—including those on your personal board of directors—handle relationships. Ask them for their wisdom and favorite readings.

In the end, all that you learn about people and life will strengthen not only your networking but also your art. How can that be anything other than a win-win situation?

– Chapter Five –

Finding Work

Where to Look, What to Ask, and How to Land the Job

There are people who don't work hard.
There are people who can't handle complex problems.
There are people who don't put in the time.
Artists are NOT those people.

—ANDREW SIMONET, *MAKING YOUR LIFE AS AN ARTIST*

I've already said how much I enjoy speaking with young artists as they are about to launch their careers. It's a way for me to keep in touch with their hopes, dreams, and their deepest concerns. Recently, when I was invited to speak to a group of seniors and graduate students at Juilliard about the business of the arts, what struck me the most was their intense anxiety about getting jobs after graduation. Indeed, I don't think it would be an exaggeration to say that they appeared to be absolutely horrified at the thought of having to consider their employment prospects for the future. So, if you are anxious, if you are worried, please know that you are not alone and that there are specific practical steps you can take to look for jobs or even create your own. But you'll need to understand beforehand what that entails.

IF AT FIRST YOU DON'T SUCCEED

We talked in Chapter 2 about the performing artist's need to deal with rejection. At this point in your journey, you've probably already navigated your way through some tough spots. After all, it's pretty much a given that all of us, no matter who we are and what we do, will face a certain amount of criticism and rejection throughout our lives. As a performing artist, however, you are likely to encounter more than most, and it is likely to be more public as well.

Just being accepted to and making it through a professional school means that, so far, you've been one of the chosen. And while on one level there may have been competition and rivalry among your fellow performers, on another you were a team, a cohesive unit working together. Criticism was generally—if not always—intended to help you improve. However, according to Sigourney Weaver, at least one of her teachers at the Yale School of Drama told her straight out that she had no talent. "You need to believe in yourself," Sigourney advises. "Don't be discouraged. Even the most well-meaning professionals may discourage you. They have a limited vision of what you can be. Don't let a teacher discourage you."

Even if you are repeatedly encouraged as a student, however, it's safe to say that once you leave the school or conservatory, you'll be facing a lot more rejection than you're probably used to. As you embark on this next step of your journey, the going gets tougher: You'll be auditioning for jobs you won't get. Your performances will be criticized in the media. How do you deal with the negative feedback?

One of the examples Sigourney gave me is a story she's told before, because the experience made such a significant impression on her. She heard the acclaimed playwright and director George Wolfe speak at a graduation ceremony at the Tisch School of the Arts, and she remembers him saying: "The single most important tool you will have in your career is failure, failure, failure." He told a story about spending a great deal of time writing a play called *Paradise*. It was completely panned. After the terrible reviews came out, he said, he walked around New York for the day and decided that he could either change what he did to make the critics happy or keep on doing what he was doing, and so he decided to keep on his own path. He likened one's career to being in a room with a series of slot machines. "You keep hearing and seeing other people winning and you don't understand why you aren't. So you think, 'well, maybe I should change machines.' He said 'Stay with your machine. It may take longer, but you will succeed.'"

The reasons for not getting a particular job can be many and various, and may have more to do with some preconceived notion or vision the person doing the hiring has already established than it does with you or your skill. Perhaps they've decided the role should be filled by a short blonde and you're a tall brunette? You could change your hair color (or wear a wig), but you can't change your height. Or maybe your partner or the person you're playing opposite has already been cast and they need someone to complement him or her. Maybe there's an opening for an alto in the chorus and you're a soprano. You may not even be aware of the reasons underlying your rejection.

But what if you do get the job and then get negative reviews? The fact is that if you're going to expose yourself to public scrutiny you'll have to find a way to cope with public response. Some performers choose not to read or listen to anything written or said about them in the media, but that can be tough—and not always the best decision, because some criticism might actually spur you to do better, even though the words or the tone can be hurtful.

The problem is now compounded by the fact that technology and social media allow everyone to be a critic—very often anonymously. Years ago, there was a limited number of critics for each art. Performers knew who they were, what their credentials were, and their particular quirks. That knowledge provided some basis for how the performer responded to the critic's, well, criticism. Now, of course, anyone can post anything in the blogosphere and the one being criticized has no way of knowing where it's coming from.

This leaves the performer having to determine which criticisms might be valid and which are merely mean-spirited. What you need to do is separate the vicious from the valid, find a way to dismiss the former, and try to depersonalize the latter (which I know isn't easy). If a criticism seems valid, listen to what's being said (or written), and use it in order to improve. Misty Copeland, the first female African American principal dancer at ABT, has had to weather some truly demeaning and inappropriate commentary by bloggers. One specific anonymous blogger engaged in what could easily be described as a racist screed. But Misty, instead of taking it personally or letting it stand in the way of her personal mission, simply reposted the blog on her Facebook page with the comment "Thoughts?" Her Facebook fans responded with vigor, and the result was twofold: not only did Misty feel supported by her fans, but they were also able to call out the blog for what it truly was—not a rational or thoughtful commentary on Misty's dancing but a prejudiced and inappropriate post—without her having to either respond directly or just "suck it up."

One thing I know for sure is this, if you fall apart each time you don't get a job or your performance is criticized, you'll be spending a lot of time curled up in a miserable ball on your sofa. You're going to need to toughen up, or else it just may be that no matter how talented you are, you're not cut out for this world. One woman with whom I danced at ABT decided after just one year in the *corps de ballet* that she could not handle the pressure of dancing with a major professional ballet company. She returned to her hometown, performed in smaller dance troupes, and ultimately became a teacher.

There are many wonderful artists who simply don't have the emotional wherewithal to deal with being a performing artist in this century. Being totally frank and realistic, I need to say that you may be incredibly talented, but if you're an emotional mess every day, you're never going to be happy. In fact, I believe this is the reason some artists become involved with alcohol or drugs. If dealing with criticism is preventing you from finding real joy in your work, it would be better to accept the harsh reality now, rather than risk going down that road. Maybe there's something else you can do that will keep you connected to the field you love but won't take the emotional toll of performing in public. Facing the truth about who you are is a brave thing to do and should never be considered a moral failing.

STARTING YOUR SEARCH

At this point, let's assume you've got a pretty good idea of who you are as a performer and how the business works. You know that it's going to be up to you to market yourself and your skills effectively in order to succeed in your chosen field. So the big question now is, to whom and where should you be directing your efforts? Or, in other words, what's the best way to find work or opportunities? And, of course, the answer is going to vary, not only among art forms but also, depending upon your area of interest and expertise, within your particular art.

If you're a dancer or singer who's been accepted in a company, an actor with a repertory group, or a musician in an orchestra or ensemble, I congratulate you, but I also urge you not to skip this chapter. Work in almost all the arts—not unlike sports—is seasonal to one degree or another. There will be times when you're on hiatus (and, therefore, effectively unemployed) and when that happens, chances are you'll be looking for gigs to fill the gaps.

But finding work is also about more than getting the job—it's about knowing what's going to be expected of you, knowing what you can or should expect of your employer, and, if you're lucky enough to have more than one opportunity, knowing which one would be best for you.

In most instances there will be some kind of agreement or contract involved, so you'll need to know what to ask for and get it in writing before you sign the dotted line. As I've said, these are responsibilities that would probably fall to an agent or manager if you had one, but, at least at the beginning of your career, that's unlikely, so chances are you'll be acting on your own behalf. And even if, down the road, you do have someone to represent you and take care of those pesky business details, the more informed you are the better you'll be able to judge whether the person you're depending upon is really doing his job.

Agents and managers handle your money, and while the vast majority of them are honest, there are also those (and unfortunately I speak from experience here) who may not be. Therefore, you need to be aware of what monies are due you and what your expenditures are, even though you may not be personally handling those transactions.

WHERE TO LOOK

Would you be surprised to hear that the best and most successful way to find work is through word of mouth? It's true, and that's why continuing to develop, expand, and maintain your board of directors and network is so important. Hands down, it is the best way to find out what is going on in your discipline in your region.

And, of course, every discipline has its own websites and publications that not only post jobs and auditions but also provide news of who's working on what new production. Maybe one of those people is someone you've met at a party or a conference. If so, now's the time to get in touch and remind him or her of your meeting. "Hi, this is Joan, we met at the X extravaganza and I just read in Y that you're going to be working on Z. Congratulations, that's great, do you know if they are still hiring? Who should I speak with?" Maybe nothing will come of it, but even if so, at least you tried. And maybe it will turn out to be your next big break.

One excellent way to introduce people to your work is to invite them to a performance. If you are doing a show or a performance, identify a few people in your field who you think might be helpful down the line and invite them! This is a chance for you to be seen in your element and strategically show what you can do.

Finally, if you are in college or a conservatory, check out your institution's career services department. That's what they're there for, and I have spoken to many college and conservatory graduates who said they regretted not having taken advantage of their own school's resources.

For better or worse, this isn't a science (it's the *arts* business). The point is to keep putting yourself out there so that serendipity will be able to find you.

Where to Look Online

Every discipline has sites where jobs are posted. Here is a sampling of those you might want to check out:

- **General**

  Art Jobs (http://artjobs.artsearch.us)

  BroadwayWorld.com (http://www.broadwayworld.com)

- **Discipline specific**

  Dance/USA (https://www.danceusa.org/jobsandauditions)

  Opera America (http://www.operaamerica.org/applications/jobs/index.aspx)

  Theatre Communications Group (http://www.tcg.org/)

  Chorus America (https://www.chorusamerica.org/jobs)

League of American Orchestras (http://www.americanorches
tras.org/career-center.html)

Actors' Equity (https://actorsequity.org)

- **Specific Companies**

Too numerous to list, virtually every arts company has its own
website that lists opportunities and job openings.

MASTERING THE AUDITION

Once you've made the connection or found out about an upcoming opportunity, whether you're a singer, a dancer, an actor, or a
musician, many jobs are going to involve some kind of audition—
the equivalent of the job interview in the civilian world, except
for the fact that job interviews are usually one-on-one while
auditions often involve large groups of job seekers performing
simultaneously or one right after the other for a potential
employer. And in some instances the "audition" may actually be
a competition. In fact, competitions for opera singers, dancers,
and musicians take place annually all over the world.

According to Rosa Lamoreaux, a professional singer and voice
teacher, competitions can help young artists to gain recognition
and get work, but winning a competition may not necessarily
lead to a job. Therefore, it is important to do both: attend auditions and enter competitions.

Sometimes the first thing you need to do is figure out which
auditions will be most likely to lead to actual employment. Otherwise you may be spending a lot of time chasing the unob-

tainable or following dead-end paths. Beyond that, you'll also be wasting your hard-earned and undoubtedly limited cash resources, because there are almost always monetary costs to looking for work. You might, for example, need to travel to the audition site. You may need to take time off from your "bill-paying job" in order to audition. The company you're auditioning for might require you to supply specialized head shots or video or audio. All of these things add up, so be mindful about which auditions are most likely to generate success. Going to every audition might make you feel that you are working "hard" (which you are), but you may not be working "smart," which is what will foster success.

> "Even when I was young, I felt that when I was auditioning, I was also auditioning the director and the other people involved in the production, and that put me in the driver's seat."
>
> —Sigourney Weaver

KNOW YOUR STRENGTHS

Laura Careless, a modern dancer, told me a very compelling story about one occasion when she decided to audition for a major modern dance company because she somehow thought she was "supposed" to get out and do every audition. As it turned out, the company danced in a style that was stylistically inconsistent with her strengths and the culture of the company made her uncomfortable. The experience was miserable.

She went home dispirited and depressed. Now she knows that she should never have set foot in that audition. It was not productive for her or for the company. It was a painful but valuable lesson, and Laura hopes that by sharing her experience she will prevent another young artist from making the same mistake.

Before you go to an audition, you need to know whom and what you're trying out for, and what the parameters are. If it's an established company of some kind, you can probably determine in advance if you'd be a good fit. And if there are physical requirements for a role, you may be able to figure that out as well. Do they want a six-foot-tall buxom blonde? A large man who can create a menacing appearance onstage? A petite ballerina to complement a not-so-tall male dancer? At ABT, the height requirements for children auditioning for *The Nutcracker* state that they must be between five feet one and five feet three, because they need to fit into the costumes already on hand. If there's no way you can even pretend to fill the bill physically, there's no point in wasting your time. Sometimes, of course, you won't know that until you're actually there, in which case all you can do is chalk it up to experience. And sometimes you won't ever know why you didn't get the job because the person doing the hiring has some physical image in his or her mind but never actually says what that is—or sometimes he doesn't know what he wants until he actually sees it.

But even assuming you have the physical appearance and the skills for a particular job, auditions are also about attributes that are far more subtle and difficult to pin down. If you're a singer, for example, it may be that your voice isn't powerful enough relative to the voices of other singers who've already been hired. Or it could be even less tangible than that. How do you comport yourself at the audition? Do you pick up directions quickly? Are you following instructions while still managing to showcase your artistic individuality and stand out from the crowd? Are you ready and able to turn on a dime, start and stop on command, and still keep your wits about you? In the director's mind, if you can do all that, you will undoubtedly be even better when you've had time to rehearse and become familiar with the material that's now being thrown at you out of the blue.

HOW NERVOUS DO YOU GET
BEFORE STEPPING ONSTAGE?

Fear, whether it be fear of change or simple stage fright, can hinder, if not paralyze, a performer. But there are also performers who say that once they step onto the stage their fear vanishes and they are "in the zone." According to Quentin Letts, writing in *The Daily Mail,* Benedict Cumberbatch, famously of PBS's *Sherlock* and the award-winning film *The Imitation Game,* has long struggled with stage fright. When he was performing in *Frankenstein* on the West End, he was "virtually vomiting from the stress every night." Obviously he has learned how to manage his stage fright, but it was clearly a significant challenge for him.

Do you think that fear pushes you to be better or prevents you from doing your best? If the latter, have you tried different ways to harness or handle your fear? A few helpful techniques might be:

- **Meditation:** Various types of meditation techniques can promote relaxation, patience, or a sense of well-being.
- **Self-affirmations:** Thinking positive or supportive thoughts can promote calm and self-confidence.
- **Talking with others:** For some people, talking through their anxieties helps to manage them.
- **Sitting or standing in silence:** Separating from others, not speaking, not engaging, helps some people to calm the mind.
- **Walking:** Walking around the block several times helps some to get the excess adrenaline out of their systems and reduces nervousness.
- **Seeing a therapist:** In certain instances it is worth seeking the help of a qualified professional therapist who can provide techniques for managing stage fright and help people work through the underlying issues that may be exacerbating the problem.

It's difficult enough to get yourself fired up for every performance even though you may be dead tired, not feeling well, or both. If, on top of that, you aren't enjoying what you're doing, the audience will sense that, and they won't be enjoying it, either.

Before giving up, you should certainly try to get some help to handle your nerves. That said, however, the truth is that some people are temperamentally more suited to live performance than others. Barbra Streisand's well-known stage fright kept her from performing live for many years. And Vladimir Horowitz, arguably one of the greatest pianists of all time, did not perform onstage or record before a live audience for more than a decade. Luckily for all of us, these great artists did eventually overcome their nerves, but there are others for whom the emotional turmoil of getting themselves onto that stage simply isn't sustainable in the long run. If you can relate to that description, you may want to focus your career on working in a recording studio, either audio or video, where you have complete control of the environment and won't have to manage the anxiety created by the immediacy of live performance.

ALWAYS BE PREPARED

Lang Lang has provided some very important advice, based on his own experience, for young people seeking work in the arts. "Always be prepared. You never know when you'll be called for an audition. Learn by heart as many pieces as possible; pieces of all periods of music. Learn at least fifteen concertos of the instrument you play. In other words, practice all the time. When you're hired, there is very limited time to learn new material but to perfect what you've learned."

In his case, being prepared led to the event that, as he put it, "transformed" his career. "It was the summer of 1999, I was seventeen. My father kept asking me to push my management company to book me for some concerts. The response from orchestras, I was repeatedly told, was that I was too young. But, one night, the phone rang. A lady I didn't know said that she had heard my audition at Carnegie Hall with the Cleveland Orchestra a few weeks earlier and wanted me to audition for Maestro Christoph Eschenbach, who was at Ravinia [America's oldest music festival and the summer home of the Chicago Symphony Orchestra] preparing for the upcoming Gala of the Century. The lady indicated that there could be a possibility of booking me later in the year.

"Delighted, my father and I took the next flight to Chicago. . . . At the audition, I played sonatas by Haydn, Brahms, Rachmaninoff, Mozart, and Beethoven, and Scriabin's études. Then, to my amazement, [the maestro] invited the executive director of Ravinia, Mr. Zarin Mehta, to the audition. He, in turn, asked me to play pieces by Schumann, Chopin, and Liszt. At the end of the audition, the maestro asked me, if I had a choice, which concerto I would play as my debut. I answered Tchaikovsky's Concerto No. 1. What should have been a twenty-minute audition lasted for nearly three hours! I was elated. My father and I returned to Philadelphia that same day.

"The following morning, the phone rang at 8 a.m. I was still half-asleep. It was my management. . . . Andre Watts, who was due to play at Ravinia that night, was sick with a fever. They needed a replacement and wanted me to play the first movement of Tchaikovsky's First Piano Concerto with the Chicago Symphony Orchestra. . . .

"At Ravinia, I peeked from my dressing room. I was told thirty thousand people were there. My time had come. With his usual charm, the great Isaac Stern came onto the stage, introduced me, and promised the audience that they wouldn't forget what they were about to hear.

"When I struck the last note of the concerto, there was a silence and then an explosion. Hearing the crowd shouting 'bravo, bravo' was overwhelming. I knew it was the beginning of something new, the beginning of a new life. And it was."

This is, of course, a wonderful story about the confluence of a great talent and a serendipitous moment, and Lang Lang speaks from the experience of a classical musician. But his lesson is applicable to any artist and any art form. You always need to be as prepared as you can be so that if and when that serendipitous moment arrives, you are ready to take advantage of it.

THE ADVANTAGE OF APPRENTICESHIPS AND FELLOWSHIPS

While auditions are generally one-shot deals (unless you get a callback), so to speak, apprenticeships and fellowships can provide you and your employer with the opportunity to get to know each other better over a period of time and determine if you're really a good fit. An apprenticeship usually involves hiring a young artist to participate in the company's activities at an introductory level. He or she may watch or participate in rehearsals, learn some entry-level roles, and get a chance to work with members of the company.

I'm a great fan of apprenticeships because I believe they're beneficial to both the performer and the company. For the company it means having more time—usually a year—to observe how you work, how you take instruction or direction, and how you fit in. From the performer's point of view, the company is making an investment of time, energy, and, many times, money in you, which means they're seriously interested in hiring you, and they're giving you a year to prove that you're worth it. It also means that you have that time to get to know the ethos of the organization and how it works, and to determine whether it's going to work for you. Beyond that, as a young artist you will also have the opportunity to learn from more experienced performers in an established, professional context.

Fellowships, on the other hand, are usually for performers who are further along in their careers. The goal of these programs is usually to strengthen an artist's skill set, help them grow to the next level, and gain experience, usually in a larger arts organization, for a period of anywhere from a few weeks or months to a year. Sometimes a fellowship will also lead to a job with the company, but that's not something you should count on. Rather, I believe you should view it as a very powerful and, many times, prestigious professional development opportunity.

Look on company websites for information about apprenticeships and fellowships. They may be listed under "education" rather than "employment," so search carefully.

TO TEACH OR NOT TO TEACH

Mark Van Doren, the renowned twentieth-century American poet and professor at Columbia University, said, "The art of teaching is the art of assisting discovery."

If you are starting out as a performer and worrying about how to support yourself while you look for work or are between performing jobs, teaching may sound like a great idea. It allows you to stay connected to your field and to others who are interested in your art form, it provides greater flexibility than any nine-to-five job, and it probably pays better than temping or waiting tables. For many people, teaching is a great alternative. But it isn't something you should enter into without serious thought.

To be a good teacher, you need to take every aspect of it seriously, and you need to be honest with yourself about whether or not you have what it takes. First of all, are you actually qualified to teach? By that I mean, have you taken courses in teaching? Do you know what it means to work with children versus teens versus adults? Have you had any pedagogical training at school? Have you worked as an assistant teacher to give you some classroom experience? Many colleges and conservatories that focus on the performing arts also have classes in arts pedagogy or education. If your school provides that opportunity, you ought to think about taking some of those courses before you leave, so that you have some understanding of the basics.

In dance, there are also teacher certification programs. You cannot assume that just because you have a degree in performance or have been playing, singing, dancing, or acting for years, you will be able to teach. It would be both irresponsible to your students and disrespectful to teaching professionals worldwide for you simply to hang up your shingle without any training and claim to be a teacher.

Beyond training, however, you also need to ask yourself if you are temperamentally suited to teach. Can you set your own ego aside and think about what is best for the student? When I was director of the Center for Dance Education at Boston Ballet, former dancers frequently came to see if they could get a job as a teacher. I was always open to the discussion, but I knew that not every wonderful dancer would also be a good teacher.

When you are a performer, you need to focus on yourself. Because the work is so demanding, performers have to think about "me, me, me," which is the antithesis of what it means to be a teacher. To be a good teacher, you need to think of the student first. It's a "you, you, you" scenario. For many performers, the transition from "me" to "you" is impossible. That does not mean they are bad people or selfish; it just means that they are not suited to the demands of being a teacher.

So again, if you think that teaching will be a great way to supplement your income, do think long and hard about whether it will be the right role for you.

CHOOSING WISELY

I'm sure that most of us, at some time in our lives, have been in the situation where we just needed a job—any job, even if it meant standing on a street corner in a chicken suit—to pay the rent. And there are also times when we've been offered jobs that might not be our first choice but pay so well that we just can't walk away. Except in such specific circumstances, however, it's important to at least consider whether a particular job is going to help solidify or, even better, advance your professional situation. I know what it feels like to just want the opportunity to do whatever it is you love and have spent your life training to do, but you don't want to sell yourself short—unless, as I've said, you're in a situation where it's a matter of survival.

Bearing that in mind, when you are considering professional opportunities, you need to be strategic and understand the costs and benefits of those opportunities. Sometimes the "costs" of taking a job that doesn't pay well are balanced by the "benefits" of being seen or working with an exceptional artist. On the one hand, you cannot do only those and survive—although when you're starting out you may need to do more of them than you would like—but no matter where you are in your career, there will always be professional opportunities you take simply because of the exposure, experience, or the prestige they provide. What you don't want to do, however, is sell yourself short and end up in an endless series of jobs that don't advance you professionally or artistically.

There are basically two ways to sell yourself short: by taking a job that doesn't use your abilities or show what you're capable of doing without providing any upside benefit, or by taking a job that doesn't pay what you believe is a fair price for your work. Be smart in your assessment of job opportunities so that you don't fall into one of these traps. There will undoubtedly be times when you should take a job that doesn't pay well because it provides a great opportunity—to work with people you admire, or to appear at an important venue to add weight to your résumé. But if you're being underpaid and your talent isn't being showcased, you are probably not making the best use of your time. In the end, as I keep saying, you need to work "smart" to get ahead. Endless and grinding work that does not move you forward artistically or financially is counterproductive.

Sometimes artists get trapped in counterproductive situations because they simply don't know or believe in their true value. Part of the reason to network with your peers as well as with those who've been around a bit longer than you, and to seek the advice of those who are in a position to do the hiring, is to get a better sense of what you're worth. In many small companies, pickup groups, or one-off gigs there are no established rates. No union is overseeing the financial terms, and there are no fixed rules about how or how much an artist is paid. In those situations it is imperative for you to be proactive, to learn about your market, and about what the going rate is for people at your level doing the kind of work you are being offered.

Virtually everyone has some bottom-line income they need to live, if not luxuriously then certainly without undue daily stress about paying the bills. In the following chapter, I'll be showing you how to determine that mathematically. The point for now is that, once you've determined what is, in effect, your baseline required income, you'll be better able to decide whether any particular job is going to pay enough to satisfy your needs.

Once you've determined your bottom line and figured out what the going rate is for your particular skills in the market-place, the other piece of the puzzle is to negotiate the terms of your work agreement—because many, although certainly not all, terms of employment are negotiable to some degree.

CONTRACTUAL INS AND OUTS

It would truly be beyond the scope of this book to provide a nuts-and-bolts, clause-by-clause, line-by-line tutorial on every aspect of every type of work agreement, but what I can do is provide some guidance on the less obvious contractual terms and obligations you might need to consider, depending upon the type of artist you are and the parameters of the gig you're signing up for. Many artists become fearful when they hear the words "negotiate a contract." Visions of used-car dealers and fast-talking salesmen dance in their heads. Don't be afraid; in truth, the goal of a negotiation is simply to come to an agreement on terms that help both parties address their needs and achieve their goals. It isn't about winning or losing, it is about finding common ground.

The first thing you should know is that, depending upon the situation, some of the terms of any contract may not be negotiable. The dates of the performance(s) may be set in stone. The salary may be the salary, and unless you have something unique to bring to the table physically or in terms of a particular skill, you may have to just take it or leave it. But in many cases you can at least ask about most things. If someone has made you an offer, they're not going to take it back just because you've tried to get a better deal. You may get a flat-out "no" for an answer, which means that you'll have to accept what was offered initially or, if it is in your mind a deal breaker, walk away, but you won't lose the job. (And if you do lose a job because you've simply asked a question or made a counteroffer, you probably shouldn't be taking that job in the first place.)

It should go without saying that any agreement must be clear about the dates of the performances or length of time of employment and the rate or amount of pay. But there are many conditions beyond salary and run of the gig to consider. Here are a few you might not have thought about on your own.

* **Transportation and lodging:** Who pays? If you're going out of town, will your airfare be paid by the company? How about transportation to and from the airport? Where will you be staying? If you're in a hotel, will you have a room to yourself? Who will be paying? What about meals? Will you receive a per diem (a particular sum for daily expenses) during the term of your employment?

  If you're touring (traveling from place to place) what kind of transportation will you be using? Who pays for your meals on the road?

* **Health insurance:** What if you get sick? Will your medical expenses be covered? If you can't work for a day or a week, will you still be paid? If not, will you receive disability payments?

* **In case of injury:** Will your medical expenses be covered? Will you be paid? Does it make a difference if you're injured on the job or simply when you're crossing the street or climbing the stairs?

* **Are there costumes or specific dress requirements?** If so, who supplies the apparel?

* **Will you be an employee or an independent contractor?** More on this in the following chapter.

* **If the performances are outdoors, what happens if there are temperature extremes?** Are you expected to perform in significant heat or cold, rain or snow?

* **What happens if one or more performances are canceled?** Do you still get paid?

* **Musicians:** Will your employer pay the cost of insuring your instrument for the run of the contract? What

happens if your instrument is damaged or lost? If you're going out of town, will your instrument need to be shipped? If so, who pays? If your instrument can't be shipped, will the company provide one for you? What kind of instrument? Do you need a Steinway piano or will any brand suffice?

* **Dancers**: What kind of venue will you be dancing in? What kind of floor will there be? Will you have to supply your own shoes?

The Proper Care and Feeding of Your Precious Instrument

If you are a musician, your instrument is probably your most precious, and also your costliest, possession. Cenovia Cummins plays on a violin made in 1716 by Giovanni Grancino of Milan. She shared with me what she knows about acquiring and taking care of her instrument.

First of all, when she tried to get a bank loan to purchase the violin in 1996, she learned that none of the nine banks she approached had a mechanism for providing instrument loans. Luckily, the Actors Federal Credit Union did provide instrument loans, and she received the funds she needed within ten days. Go to their website to see if you are eligible to join (actorsfcu.com).

Cenovia also advises that generally:

1. The interest on an instrument loan is tax deductible.
2. If you are in an orchestra, the orchestra will pay for instrument insurance, but if you are self-employed you will have to pay it yourself.

---

3. Get the best insurance you can for your instrument. The cost of your instrument insurance (if you pay it yourself) is tax deductible.

4. You can depreciate the value of your instrument on your income taxes even though the instrument itself may be appreciating in value.

5. If you are flying with your instrument you will have to purchase a separate plane ticket for it. If it's large (like a cello, for example) you'll also have to get it a seat belt extender. And you'll also have to make sure you get a bulkhead (larger) seat.

HAVE YOUR PAPERS IN ORDER

There's a reason why men and women in the chorus are traditionally known as gypsies, but, more and more these days, all kinds of performers must be ready, willing, and able to pack a bag and hit the road at any moment. And that often means traveling to a different country, with all the paperwork and preparation that entails. Working artists get to see a lot of the world, which means that, to be a savvy performer, you need to keep your passport up to date, make sure you have any inoculations that might be required, and know how and where to get a visa if necessary (and find out if the company will help or get it for you).

All of this can be even more complicated if you are not a citizen of the country whose organization is hiring you, so it would be wise to find out in advance what you'll need to do should the situation arise. You never want to have to pass up a job because your paperwork isn't in order.

Decoding Work Permits and Visas

If you are a United States citizen and want to work in another country, chances are you will need to get a work permit from that country to do so.

Work permits are different from visas. A visa is a document from a country that allows you to enter the country for a specific amount of time and under specific conditions. A work permit is legal authorization from a country's government for a noncitizen to take a job within that country.

Many countries—including all of Europe, the United Kingdom, and Canada, as well as many countries in Central and South America—do not require tourists to get a visa in advance. Basically, the stamp you get on your passport when you enter the country is your visa. Virtually all countries, however, do require you to obtain a work permit in order to take a job. When ABT toured (and we have gone everywhere from Abu Dhabi to China to Russia) we had to secure a work visa/permit for *every* member of the company who was traveling and working on that tour. Similarly, when performing arts companies from other countries come to The Music Center to perform, generally speaking, they are responsible for getting U.S. visas for all of their workers. Doing that can be complicated, time-consuming, and expensive.

Here are two important things to keep in mind if you are considering or have been offered a job working abroad:

1. If you are touring with a group, be sure the company or tour organizer has obtained the necessary work visas/permits for everyone who is traveling. If anyone says you can work on a tourist visa, they are wrong. In fact, if you do not have the proper visa or work permit, chances are that you simply will not be paid for your work.

2. Each country has its own rules, although there are some basic characteristics all work permits share:
   - Work permits are for one specific job from one employer only.
   - Work permits have a predetermined time limit.
   - Work permits are issued at the discretion of the government and can be changed or revoked at any time.
   - Most countries require that you apply for a work permit before you leave home, not after you arrive.

THE ART OF THE INTERVIEW

So you've found a job and received some great reviews—even more wonderful opportunities lie ahead for you, and you may be asked to give an interview. Newspapers, magazines, radio, and television allow you to be "heard" by a large and diverse segment of the population. If you present yourself well, these are opportunities to bring greater recognition to your brand and introduce new audiences to your work. Therefore, you need to be prepared; don't figure you'll just "wing it." I'm sure you've read articles or seen people on television and wondered what the interviewee could have been thinking when he said this or that, because he came off sounding mean-spirited, ignorant, or just plain silly—and you know him, so you know he's not really like that at all.

From your first contact with a producer or a journalist to your last handshake, all interviews provide extraordinary opportunities for you to introduce yourself to a broad audience, which is why it's so important to present your brand at its very best.

How to Prepare for and Manage
a Newspaper or Magazine Interview

* Before the interview takes place—even before you agree to do it—ask the writer about the content of the article. Will this be a profile? Are they asking for an opinion about your field? Try to find out if they have any knowledge of the arts, and of your discipline specifically. Why have they come to you as opposed to someone else in your field? What does the writer want to know—and why? Does he or she have an agenda, and, if so, consider whether it is something you really want to talk about in public.

* Do some research on the publication in which the article will appear. If it is the *New York Times,* you know it is a credible organization; if it's a known tabloid or completely unknown to you, you need to find out what the publication is about (buy a copy or read it online), who the writer is (look up articles she's had published in the past), and then decide if you really want to participate. Don't just grab at the opportunity, but don't turn it down, either, until you are as well informed as possible.

* Draft some talking points. Once you know the nature of the publication, tailor your talking points to its core audience and think about how you can engage them in what you have to say about your work. Magazines in particular may have very targeted audiences, and you should keep that demographic in mind as you form your responses. I say this from personal experience, because once, when I was being interviewed for a profile in *Vogue* magazine, I was going on and on about being an arts leader, the mis-

sion of American Ballet Theatre, and the future of professional dance, until, about two-thirds of the way through the interview, the wonderful writer stopped me and said, "Rachel, this is *Vogue*. We are a fashion magazine. I think we now need to talk about clothes and fashion!" While I was perfectly aware that the article was going to be on fashion, I got so involved in what I was saying that I forgot my audience. The writer's comment brought me back to reality, and the memory of that experience still serves to remind me how important it is to keep a publication's focus and intended audience in mind during an interview.

How to Prepare for and Manage a Television or Radio Appearance

* Once you've agreed to do the interview, create a folder containing all the details of the appearance. Who are your contacts; what are the topics, time, and location?

* Follow all the instructions provided by the producer or contact. What to wear, what to bring with you, and so on.

* Watch a few episodes of the show to understand its format, tone, segment lengths, and how the host or interviewer interacts with guests. How prepared is he or she? Does she have notes in front of her? How extemporaneous does he appear?

* Do draft some key talking points, but don't memorize a speech. You want to appear natural, not overrehearsed and stiff. Depending on the size of the station, a staff member

might call you in advance to work out what you'll be talking about. But that probably won't happen if it's a smaller, local station.

* Arrive early so that you have time to get the lay of the land, so to speak, and introduce yourself to the staff. Again, at larger outlets there will probably be someone to greet you, but smaller ones may not have this arrangement, which means you'll have to find your own way.

* Be yourself. Listen to what is being said and respond authentically to the questions. Remember that this is a conversation, a give-and-take. It's not a deposition. Every interviewer's nightmare is the guest who answers "yes" or "no" and then doesn't offer anything more. And, as always when speaking before the public, take the "high road," even if the interviewer is subtly, or not-so-subtly, pressing you to do otherwise. Being boastful or putting others down will not endear you to the audience, and potential employers will not see you as someone they would want to represent their organization.

* As soon as possible—preferably that same day—send a thank-you note to the producer. Being thoughtful and appreciative will help you stand out.

* If you're a member of a company, you'll need to let your employers know if you're going to be discussing their business. But even if you're not going to be discussing company business, it would be a good idea to let them know about the interview

in advance. For one thing, they may be able to give you good and useful advice, and, for another, you'll be forewarned if there are topics to avoid or if, for some reason you might not be aware of, you should decline that particular appearance.

* Find out how to get a copy of the interview for your own use. Be mindful that there might be copyright issues, so ask how you will be allowed to use the material. Can you post it on your Facebook page and/or your personal website? If you are employed by a company, can you give it to the marketing department to post on their website? Find out how to get permissions in case you might want to use a clip for professional purposes at some time in the future.

YOU CAN DO THIS

I know that much of what I've been saying may sound daunting and cause you to feel overwhelmed. But I want to make a strong point about artists and work that I hope will make you feel better: *You already have the skills you need to succeed,* even if you don't know it yet.

When I was working at Boston Ballet, I used to visit local Chamber of Commerce meetings and speak to local businesspeople about the value of hiring dancers. Dancers, like all performers, are disciplined, dedicated problem solvers who can work singly or in groups. They understand deadlines and are incredibly resilient.

As an artist, the skills you already employ in practicing your craft will also help you to navigate the "business side" of the artist's life. Quite simply, you wouldn't have made it as far as you have in your training or career if you weren't creative, diligent, and disciplined. You've just got to believe in yourself and go for it.

So take heart and take control; successful artists don't wait for doors to be opened for them or jobs to be handed to them on a silver platter—they are entrepreneurial in spirit and create their own opportunities.

Chapter Six

How to Be Financially Smart from the Start

Taxes, Insurance, and Other Important Survival Smarts

The most common money-related mistake
artists make is a reluctance to invest in their own careers."
—*CAROLL MICHELS, ART MARKETING CONSULTANT AND CAREER COACH*

So the good news is you've got a job; the bad news is that it may not be a long-term job, or, even if it is, it might not pay very well. Young—and even seasoned—performers often find themselves struggling to make ends meet. I know I did as a young dancer, sharing a studio apartment with two roommates and considering a jar of peanut butter a major but worthwhile investment because it was nutritious and almost infinitely spreadable.

At the time, any windfall was almost like winning the lottery. I still remember one very unexpected gift I received when I went to buy a new pair of pointe shoes. I was not yet a member of the company and, therefore, had to buy my own shoes. They cost seventy-five dollars, which was an enormous amount of money for me, especially since I had to replace them at least every couple of weeks. On this particular day I was wearing a truly ratty pair of sneakers, and the very polite British salesman who was helping me drew my attention to an extremely stylish pair of jazz shoes. (Was that some kind of subtle hint about the condition of my footwear?) I assured him that the shoes were beautiful, and of course I'd love to own them, but I couldn't possibly afford them. When I got to the cash register to pay for my pointe shoes, there was a second box waiting for me—a deeply treasured gift from a stranger I'll never forget.

While it's lovely to receive an unexpected gift with no strings attached, there's really nothing romantic (with apologies to Signore Puccini) about living *la vie bohème,* worrying about where the rent is going to come from month after month, having to put up with a roommate (or roommates) you don't really get along with, or taking job after job just because you have to. It may be true that money doesn't buy happiness, but it can buy a certain degree of freedom from at least one kind of stress. Being constantly stressed about money can be draining and distracting, and not having enough can prevent you from affording the additional training that might get you to the next level as an artist (and, therefore, the next level on the pay scale as well).

If you're not as savvy as you'd like to be about money and are struggling financially, you are far from being the exception. In fact, a 2012 survey of 1,307 men and women ages 25 to 59 found that credit card debt and problems sticking to a budget were the two main factors preventing the study subjects from achieving their monetary goals. Unfortunately, money management is a skill for which most of us do not have any formal training. And since the majority of performers—even those who are well established—may well have to be vigilant about spending and saving throughout their careers, you would be wise to get smart about money from the start.

The first step is really to figure out what you're going to need to live on—your no-frills bottom line, so to speak. Andrew Simonet of Artists U has a great formula for how to do that:

First: Understand what you spend your money on. Write down everything you spend money on for a week. You might be surprised by what you spend without ever thinking about it, which could help you to reallocate the limited funds that you do have. For instance, can you start eating breakfast at home instead of grabbing an Egg McMuffin? Can you review your cell phone plan and possibly find a less expensive one? Are you using a credit card to fund "splurges"?

Second: Look at your most recent tax return and write down the number on the line marked "gross income." This is the amount you earned *before* taxes were taken out. Add to that any money you earned that was not taxable (and therefore not included on your tax return), such as money from scholarships or fellowships or gifts of up to $14,000 (as of 2015; the figure increases annually).

Third: Think about your last year. Were you able to manage with the cash you had? Did you have trouble paying bills? Getting groceries? Covering other essentials such as health insurance? Setting aside some savings? In other words, did you make enough to live a sustainable lifestyle? Be honest with yourself, and if you determine that you need more, add that number to your previous year's gross income. On the other hand, be realistic about what you can expect to earn. If you happen to have a windfall, that's great, but don't count on it!

Fourth: Divide your final number by 1,500 to get the amount you would need to make if you were being paid by the hour. (Technically, you would divide your final number by 2,080, which is 40 hours/week x 52 weeks, but this does not allow for any illness, injury, or downtime. The 1,500 number builds in some of that.) This is your hourly rate. Once you have an hourly rate, multiply it by 8 to get your daily rate, and multiply your daily rate by 5 to get your weekly rate. Your weekly rate multiplied by 52 should equal the number you came up with as the minimum gross income you need to live on.

DEALING WITH DEBT

I'm going to start from the premise that most of you are emerging from your respective schools and conservatories with some degree of debt. This will probably be one of your greatest financial challenges as you build a sustainable artistic career.

According to nerdwallet.com, the average student loan debt is $32,264, and that number seems to go up every year. But even if you are one of the lucky few who manage to graduate debt-free, you're not completely out of the woods yet and you still need to be wary of starting to accrue debt that you may have a hard time paying off later.

Know Your Credit Score

If you ever want to buy or lease a car, buy a house, or, many times, even rent an apartment, the seller will look at your credit report to determine whether you are a "good risk." The report includes information on where you live, whether you pay your bills on time, the amount of debt you already have, and whether you have ever been sued or have filed for bankruptcy. Based on this information, you are then assigned a credit score. Nationwide credit reporting companies sell the information in your report to creditors, insurers, employers, and other businesses that use it to evaluate your application for a loan, a mortgage, a credit card, insurance, or the lease on a house or apartment.

The Fair Credit Reporting Act requires each of the nationwide credit reporting companies (Equifax, Experian, and TransUnion) to provide a *free* copy of your credit report every twelve months. It is important to look at your credit report and see if there are any errors or issues you need to resolve before they come back to haunt you later. For a free report, go to www.annualcreditreport.com or call 1-877-322-8228.

Here's the thing about debt: It tends to keep mounting up. And it sneaks up on you gradually. You're short on cash because you have to pay at least the minimum on your credit card bill(s), which means that you charge more stuff because you don't have the cash to pay for it, which then increases the minimum amount you need to pay on next month's credit card bill. If you get behind, your interest rate goes up and your credit score goes down. But here's the catch—if you pay just the minimum amount on time, your credit card company will love you (because they're collecting a lot of interest for doing absolutely nothing), and they will increase your credit limit, thereby tempting you to charge even more. It's really easy for that debt to become overwhelming, and overwhelmingly difficult to get out from under.

According to Lucy Duni, vice president of consumer education at TrueCredit.com by TransUnion, the balance you owe on your credit card should be less than 35 percent of your available credit.

Some Helpful Financial Hints

- Have only one credit card and use it only when you absolutely have to, such as to rent car, reserve a hotel room, or to buy a plane ticket. But keep your charges to an absolute minimum.

- Use a debit card, cash, or PayPal to make your purchases. All of these come out of your checking account, so you won't be able to spend money you don't have. Open your financial mail (especially your bills and you bank statements) right away. You need to know what these documents say, even if it is not pretty.

- Pay your bills *as soon as possible*. Don't wait until the due date. That's how you can get to be late on your payments, which will negatively impact both your credit rating and the interest you'll be paying in the future.

- Pay your bills online. This is a fast, easy, and cheap way to manage your finances. You won't have to buy stamps, *and* you'll have a record of the transaction.

- Keep all your financial papers (bills, receipts, pay stubs) in one place. Be disciplined and put them in their "home" right away. This will keep you somewhat organized for when you have to do your taxes or look something up for some reason.

I'm not here to lecture. I know how hard it is to keep your head above water, particularly if, like so many young performers, you're living in an expensive city because that's where the work is, and you're earning very little, or, at times, nothing at all. Still, the more aware you are of your financial obligations and how they relate to what's going to be in your paycheck, the better prepared you will be to create some kind of realistic budget you can live with (and on), and hopefully even put a little aside to have on hand when a need or an opportunity arises.

If you do have student loan debt, those payments should be at the top of your "need to pay" list, right after rent and food. But you also—truly—need to start creating a little nest egg and—difficult as it may be for you to think about when you're just starting out—planning for your retirement. And then there's insurance: health insurance first and foremost, as well as long-term disability, renter's insurance (if you're renting a place to live), and, if you're a musician, insurance for your instrument and/or other expensive electronic equipment.

To do any of the above, the first thing you'll need to know is how much money will be coming in—and often even that is difficult to determine.

WHAT'S IN YOUR PAYCHECK?

The answer to that question is, "It depends." It depends on whether you're an employee or an independent contractor. And if you're an employee, it depends on whether you're contributing to the cost of health insurance or any other pretax deductions your employer may be offering, such as a 401(k) or even the cost of a MetroCard. Already confused? I'm not surprised. Let's try to decode some of those initials on your paycheck that explain why the amount you were told you'd be earning per week is significantly more than the amount you're actually receiving.

Your Paycheck Decoded

- **FICA:** You may never have heard of the Federal Insurance Contributions Act, but I bet you've heard of Social Security. FICA is the amount deducted from your paycheck so that you'll receive Social Security payments when you reach retirement age (even if you don't actually retire). There is a cap on the amount of earnings subject to Social Security tax, but in 2015 it was $118,500.00, so unless you're very lucky, you won't even have to think about that right away. Your FICA deduction also includes money that goes toward paying for Medicare and federal disability payments. Your employer pays a share that is equal to yours.

- **Income tax withholding:** Your employer is required by law to withhold a certain amount from your paycheck to "prepay" the amount of federal, state, and (if applicable) local income tax you will owe, based on your salary and the self-declared number of deductions you elect to take. For most of you that will be about one-third of your salary. When you're hired, you are asked to fill out a form stating the number of deductions (also called allowances) you want to take from the total tax you will owe on your salary. Basically, if you are single and have only one job, taking one allowance (yourself) should result in your breaking even at the

---

end of the year—meaning that you shouldn't owe any additional taxes but you also probably won't get a refund. Beyond that, other factors—being married, having children, being responsible for an adult dependent—will all play into determining the appropriate number of allowances to take. What you need to know, however, is that there will be taxes withheld from your paycheck, and the amount will be based on a) your gross (that is, pretax) salary and b) the number of deductions (allowances) you choose to take. In January your employer will send you a W-2 form, which indicates your total income as well as the total amount of tax that was withheld in the previous year. If you have more than one job, you may receive more than one W-2 form. A copy of this form also goes to the Internal Revenue Service. So, as my mother always said when I was growing up, "Never monkey with the IRS!"

- **Pretax deductions:** In addition to FICA and income tax withholding, there may be other deductions taken from your salary before you receive your paycheck. These are taken before your income tax withholding is calculated (which is why they're called pretax deductions), and that means you won't be taxed on the amount being deducted. Among the most common of these:

  - Your contribution to health insurance. Gone are the good old days when most employers paid 100 percent of their employees' health insurance costs. Now almost all employees must contribute something to that cost. There are often several options among which you can choose, and depending on the level of coverage you elect, the cost will vary.

- Contributions to a 401(k), a 403(b) (if you work for a non-profit), or another type of retirement plan. You don't have to put money into a 401(k) or 403(b) even if your company offers it, but if the company has a matching policy, meaning that for every dollar you put in they will put in an equal amount or some fraction of that amount, it would really be to your benefit to try to do it—even if it's only 1 percent of your salary—because your employer is, in effect, offering you "free money." This money isn't being taken away from you; it's just being invested for you so that it accrues over time and is, in effect, making money for you to use later. Unlike the money that's deducted for your health insurance, you will have to pay taxes on this money when you actually receive it. Meanwhile, however, it will be reducing the total amount on which you have to pay income tax.

IF YOU'RE NOT A FULL-TIME EMPLOYEE

If you're an independent contractor, meaning that you're working gigs rather than being a member of a company, your personal financial obligations can be even more complicated. You need to be absolutely clear about what your status is before you take a job. If you have any doubt, ask! Any responsible businessperson will regard it as a sensible question.

Get It in Writing

A Verbal Contract Isn't Worth the Paper It's Written On

Whether you're a full-time employee or an independent contractor, it's important to get the terms of your employment in writing. While I believe that most people are honest, and I don't want to plant unnecessary seeds of suspicion, I do believe that having a piece of paper that lays out the terms of any agreement is the best way to avoid a possible misunderstanding down the road. And the same holds true if you are the person doing the hiring.

The agreement should cover the obligations of both parties and what recourse either would have if the other party failed to live up to his or her part of the agreement, failed to pay the agreed-upon fee in a timely fashion, or failed to produce a product that lived up to the other's expectation.

The situation you never want to be in is a "he said/she said" argument with an employer or an employee that will at best lead to unnecessary stress and bad feelings on both sides and at worst to some kind of forced arbitration or legal action.

1099S AND ALL THAT

Independent contractors do not generally have income taxes deducted from their paychecks, but that doesn't mean that free-lancers don't have to pay taxes. On the contrary, it becomes your responsibility to make sure you *do* pay taxes. What happens is that, at the end of the year (or, most likely the beginning of the following year), everyone for whom you've done a job and from whom you've received payment of $600 or more will send you a Form 1099, which states the amount you've been paid and whether or not any taxes have been withheld from that amount. A copy of the form is also sent to the IRS (just like a W-2 for employees)—so, in effect, the government knows you've been paid that money and expects to receive the amount of tax you owe on the income. That said, do not assume that if you don't receive a 1099 from someone you don't have to pay taxes on that money. The person who paid you may have informed the IRS even if he didn't send you a 1099. So not paying could wind up costing you more in interest and penalties in the end.

It's then up to you to calculate your own taxes (or hire someone to do it for you), and to pay the proper amount to the proper agencies in timely fashion (that is, by April 15—unless April 15 happens to fall on a Sunday or a national holiday, in which case you'll get a one-day grace period).

ESTIMATED TAXES

After the first year, if you continue to work as an independent contractor, you'll have to pay estimated taxes. What this means is that, based on the amount you earned the previous year, you will have to prepay your taxes quarterly (returns are generally due on or by these dates: April 15, July 15, October 15, and January 15). If you underpay, you'll owe more the following April; if you overpay, you'll get a refund and the government will either send you a check or apply your overpayment to next year's taxes (the choice is yours). It can be difficult to guess exactly right—

that is, to estimate with complete accuracy—but as long as your estimated tax payments are equal to the amount of tax you owed the previous year you won't be penalized for underpaying, even if you make a lot more than you'd estimated.

The point is that if you're an independent contractor, the burden is on you. No one is going to do it for you—unless or until you're doing well enough to hire a business manager or an accountant or both.

SEASONAL EMPLOYEES WHO
ALSO WORK INDEPENDENTLY

Particularly in the performing arts, this is a fairly common situation. Many companies work on a "season" and then go on hiatus until the beginning of the next season. At ABT, for example, dancers are on a thirty-six-week annual contract. This means that ABT pays its dancers as employees during their "workweeks," and they are in effect unemployed for sixteen weeks of every year. If that's your situation you can either collect unemployment insurance or take other gigs during your layoff period.

Some organizations, like ABT, provide contracts based on time. Others write contracts based on service. For example, all performers at the Los Angeles Opera have union contracts, but those contracts may be "per service," meaning that the performer is under contract either for a given production or for a particular length of time. While there are some "seniority" provisions for long-standing performers in the orchestra or chorus, all performers must be prepared for the reality that they will be making more or less money—because they have more or less work—from one year to another.

Unemployment insurance provides people who are unemployed with funds that will at least partially replace their wages for a period of twenty-six weeks (plus possible extensions). Performers who are laid off are eligible to receive unemployment benefits if a) they are able to work; b) they are unemployed through no fault of their own (meaning that they were not fired for cause and did not quit); and c) they are actively seeking other work.

The amount paid by unemployment insurance varies from state to state but is always based on a percentage of the salary you were earning, and there is also a weekly cap that, again, varies from one state to another. Since the amount you receive is less than what you were earning, and the income is taxable, most performers on hiatus either look for gigs or teach during their layoff periods. That income, too, is taxable and will have to be reported and included in your estimated taxes for the year.

GETTING SERIOUS ABOUT INSURANCE

Yes, I know, you're young, you're healthy, and you think nothing bad is ever going to happen to you. And believe me, I hope you're right about that. But that's why people have insurance—so that when the thing they never imagined would happen actually does, they'll have the money they need to weather the storm. It certainly had never occurred to me when I was eighteen that I was going to fall while I was auditioning and fracture my foot before I was even accepted at ABT, or that, six years later, I would reinjure the same foot so badly that I would have to stop dancing. Of course, as a dancer I was more vulnerable to injury than, say, a pianist or an opera singer, but the point is that anyone can get sick or be injured at any time. It doesn't have to be job-related but it can certainly impact your ability to do your job, and, in any case, you need to be able to pay for the medical attention you need when you need it—it's not something you can put off until you save up for it.

We've already talked about the fact that, if you're a company employee, some portion of the cost of health insurance will be deducted from your paycheck. But the flip side of that coin is that you know your medical bills will be covered if you're injured or ill, which gives you a kind of safety net that allows you to take chances that will ultimately help you to improve your art.

Health insurance, in my opinion, would be a "must have" even if it were not now legally mandated. There are many options for the level of coverage you choose (and can afford) and many places to go to discover what those options are. There's your employer, of course, if you're a full-time employee, and your union, if you belong to one. But there are also other organizations whose mission it is to advise and empower performing artists in many areas of their lives, including health insurance. Two that are national in scope are:

* **The Actors Fund's Artists Health Insurance Resource Center.** Don't be fooled by the name: the Actors Fund welcomes people from all areas of the performing arts.
* **Fractured Atlas** is an organization devoted to providing all kinds of practical information and help to individual performing artists and arts organizations, including health insurance.

Also, I would strongly suggest that anyone who can legally remain on their parents' health insurance (as I luckily was when I fractured my foot) do so for as long as possible. For one thing, if your parent or parents are employed full-time, their insurance may be better and possibly less expensive than what you would be able to afford on your own. And even if they ask you to reimburse them for the cost of insuring an additional dependent, you will probably still be saving money.

Workers' Compensation Insurance vs. Health Insurance

If you are an employee who is injured on the job, your injury should be covered by workers' compensation insurance, not your personal health insurance. Workers' comp is a form of insurance paid for by the employer that provides wage replacement and medical benefits to employees who are injured during the course of employment. In exchange, the employee must relinquish his or her right to sue the employer for negligence.

In addition to medical insurance, I believe very strongly that everyone ought to have long-term disability insurance. Like health insurance, this is, in my opinion, vitally important, because if you are injured or have an illness that makes working impossible, you can be absolutely decimated financially. Long-term disability insurance provides you with benefits that replace a portion of your wages if you are seriously ill or injured. In the United States, the average length of time an individual on disability is out of work is 2.5 years. Imagine if you couldn't work for 2.5 years! What would that do to you or your family?

Long-term disability is generally available through your employer at very little cost but is, unfortunately, more expensive to get as an individual. If you are employed, ask your employer if it is available; it could truly save your future.

Other types of insurance that I would recommend everyone have if it is at all possible are renter's insurance and insurance for any expensive equipment you might need or use professionally.

If you don't own very much that is of significant value, you might wonder why you would need renter's insurance at all. But in fact it covers a lot more than the theft or loss of personal property from your home—although I would assume that you'd like to be able to replace lost or stolen articles should they go missing. In any case, your renter's insurance will also cover you for liability should someone injure themselves in your home and seek to hold you legally responsible for their medical and/or other expenses resulting from that injury. *Oh but my friends would never do that to me*, you say. *Never say never* is my answer, and, in any case, I'm sure there have been or will be people in your home whom you don't know that well. At a party maybe, or a friend of your roommate? Beyond personal liability, however, your insurance will also cover the cost of damage done by fire or flood—to your apartment or to one of your neighbor's. If a pipe bursts, that is the landlord's responsibility, but if you mistakenly leave the water running in the sink and it overflows and floods the apartment downstairs, your neighbor's insurance company will negotiate with your insurance company (if you have one) for damages. If you don't have insurance, you may be personally responsible for repairing the damage you caused.

Again, insurance is not for the things you expect to happen; it's for those times when the unexpected pops up and takes you by surprise.

Finally, there's the insurance you really should have—and in some cases may be required to have—for your professional equipment. Particularly if you travel with sound equipment or with an instrument, it could be lost, stolen, or damaged. If you can't afford to replace it, you also won't be able to work. Could there be a more vicious circle than that? Therefore, if you've taken a bank loan to pay for your expensive instrument or equipment, the bank may require you to insure it—because they want to be sure you'll be able to replace it and keep working so that you can keep making your payments.

TURNING EXPENSES INTO DEDUCTIONS

After talking about all the insurance you may be paying for yourself, you'll no doubt be happy to know that the cost of your health insurance—assuming you personally pay the premiums—is tax deductible. Premiums paid by your employer, even if they come out of your paycheck, are not deductible because they've already been deducted from your taxable income in those pretax dollars we discussed earlier.

In addition, if you are self-employed (and in some instances even if you are a full-time employee) there are many expenses related to your performance career that you may be able to take as tax deductions.

I don't pretend to be an expert in tax law, but here are a few major categories of potentially deductible expenses you should look into. Some of these include:

* Dues paid to unions or other professional organizations
* Classes you take to improve/advance your professional expertise
* Travel expenses (other than local travel) you incur in order to perform that are not otherwise reimbursed
* Clothing or footwear you must buy specifically for performance
* Equipment you must buy in order to do your job
* Musical scores, if you're a musician or a singer
* Marketing materials such as head shots, business cards, flyers, brochures, etc.

It's best to know about these as soon as possible because, in order to take the deductions you could be entitled to, you'll have to keep records and, in many instances, actual receipts to support the expenditures. If you think you might be eligible to take any of these, it might well be worth your while to consult an accountant or tax preparer who specializes in the performing arts and, therefore, could provide you with information about a treasure trove of potential deductions you might never have thought of yourself—as well as warn you against those that might raise a red flag with the IRS.

Financial Record-Keeping in the Electronic Age

We're lucky to be living in a time when it's easy to keep good financial records without drowning under a mound of paper. We just need to keep current, remember to enter expenses and receipts into our virtual files, and get rid of the papers we no longer need. Here are a few tips to help you get started.

- Once you get an annual statement from a company (including credit cards, banks, and pay stubs), get rid of the monthlies or weeklies. You do not need them, and they take up space. Once you receive a W-2, shred or trash your pay stubs.

- Keep your online receipts in a financial folder. Scan or take a picture of paper receipts with your phone and add them to your financial folder.

- Convert emailed financial statements into PDFs. They are easy to file and view on your computer, and they will be accessible when you need to do your end-of-year tax prep.

- Scan or photocopy hard-to-replace documents such as insurance agreements, receipts from major purchases, rental leases, and *anything* that had to be notarized, and put them in an IN CASE OF EMERGENCY folder on your computer.

- Hang on to tax returns for seven years, in case you need to make changes or happen to be audited. You can save these electronically as well. This is especially easy if you file your taxes electronically.

- Finally, make sure all of your documents are safe by acquiring a backup system for your computer. There are "cloud" services that are free or cost less than ten dollars a month if you want more "bells and whistles." This is a critical safeguard. The rule of thumb in the electronic world is that if something does not exist in three places, it does not exist as all. Losing your data is not an "if," it is a "when." So, save the data on your computer; store it on an external drive or USB "memory" stick, *and* store it with a cloud service.

GET SAVVY ABOUT SAVING

I'm totally aware of the fact that when you're barely making ends meet it's hard to conceive actually putting money aside and, therefore, living on even less. That said, I'm also painfully aware of how important it is to have access to some cash when things go wrong or, conversely, when an unexpected opportunity arises.

I've already said that the residuals I received from a commercial in which I appeared when I was still dancing helped to pay my college tuition after injury brought my dancing career to a sudden end. But there may also be times when good things come your way that require a cash outlay up front. You might, for example, be asked to appear in a production taking place in some fabulously exotic location. You'll be paid for your work, but first you have to get there. If you don't have the money for the airfare (which will later be tax deductible) you might miss out on a great opportunity.

The question, of course, is where to get the money. I'm not saying it's easy, but every little bit helps. Recently, I saw a news story about a woman who was starting to save for her young child's college tuition by never spending her change. Every day she'd come home and take all the change out of her purse and put it in a jar.

When the jar was full, she put it in the bank. Even that change adds up more quickly than you'd imagine. So while your purse gets lighter (and easier to carry), your savings account gets heftier.

Some people have a $5 jar. Every time they get a $5 bill, they put it in the jar. You'd be amazed at how those fivers can add up over time. (And no cheating by asking for your change in singles!)

If you are an employee, you may want to ask your employer about direct deposit of your paycheck. That way you can have a portion go into a savings account before you ever "see" it, which will make it a lot less painful.

Or perhaps, as I did with those commercials, you've had the opportunity to earn some extra money outside of your regular work. I know it's tempting to spend that little windfall after you've been scrimping for so long just to get by. So, by all means, take yourself out for a nice dinner or buy a new pair of shoes, but then put the rest of the money in the bank, hopefully in some kind of interest-bearing account.

Whatever money you set aside will still be there for you if you really need it, but that also means you'll be more likely to dip into it. So, saving for the long-term or for retirement might mean that you should also try to put some money in a place where you can't get to it so easily—such as that 401(k) or 403(b) we discussed earlier or an individual retirement account (IRA).

The maximum you can put into an IRA per year is now $5,000, but perhaps more important to you, you can also put in as little as you want—or just as much as you can afford, and you don't have to do it in one lump sum. You can make multiple contributions throughout the year. Putting money in an IRA will reduce your tax burden because that money isn't taxable until you take it out.

But if you do take it out before you reach the age of fifty-nine and a half, you'll not only owe the taxes on that money but will also have to pay a penalty for "early withdrawal." That's the government's way of creating an incentive for you to save long-term!

For those of you who are interested in learning even more about managing your finances as well as balancing your artistic and financial goals, I suggest you check out the financial services offered by the Actors Fund (http://www.actorsfund.org/services-and-programs/financial-wellness-program). They can help you with a lot more than simply your health insurance needs.

ARTISTS REALLY ARE GOOD WITH MONEY

While trying to digest all this information all at once can be daunting, I want you to know that, contrary to popular belief, artists are really good with money. As a former board chairman of ABT used to say, "Poverty focuses the mind." Because artists do not generally have access to huge financial reserves, they are compelled to be incredibly creative and resourceful.

You may not want making money to be the goal that drives your work and life plan, but you do need be mindful of where it's coming from and where it's going. You need to apply some of the grit, determination, and focus that drive you artistically to being a savvy, responsible money manager. The more knowledge you have now, the less you'll have to worry about it, and, therefore, the more energy you'll be able to devote to your art.

Chapter Seven

When Things Go Wrong

How to Prepare, Where to Go, What to Do

The difference between stumbling blocks
and stepping-stones is how you use them.

—AUTHOR UNKNOWN

Things go wrong in every life and every business. No one is exempt. Just knowing that and understanding there are places you can go, things you can do, and people you can talk to when the going gets rough puts you ahead of the game.

The most important thing I urge you to do—and I can't emphasize this enough—is to pay close attention to all the financial information in the previous chapter and make yourself as bulletproof as possible, so that if you are laid off, sick, injured, or just plain out of work, you'll have the wherewithal to get through those lean times with as few battle scars as possible. Having said that, financially and otherwise there will always be times when the unexpected and/or uninvited rears its ugly head.

BE SURE YOU
UNDERSTAND WHAT YOU'RE SIGNING

On the simplest level, it could be that an employer, or a potential employer, is not being as forthcoming as he or she should be about his expectations or your compensation. I must say—if I haven't said it already—that the majority of people in the performing arts business are caring and honest, but just as in any business, you may run into someone who isn't.

If you're handed a contract or a work-for-hire agreement that doesn't seem to say what you were verbally promised, and if the person hiring you can't or won't explain it to your satisfaction, *don't sign it*. If you happen to have a good friend or a family member who is an attorney, great. By all means consult that person. But if you don't, you can turn to Volunteer Lawyers for the Arts, an organization with chapters throughout the country whose mission is to "provide pro bono arts-related legal representation to low-income individual artists and nonprofit arts organizations." And the same would hold true if you were the one buying goods or services—such as publicity photos or other marketing materials, music, or costumes—from somebody else. Make sure you know what you're supposed to be getting, how you'll be able to use it, and what it's going to cost.

In the electronic age, we're all accustomed to simply clicking "I agree" whenever one of those lists of terms shows up in tiny type on a website, but when it comes to signing off on your livelihood, that's probably not the best way to approach it.

IF YOU'RE HARASSED OR DISCRIMINATED
AGAINST IN THE WORKPLACE

It happens—hopefully not to you, but it happens. If you're young, struggling, and need the job, you may be reluctant to report misconduct on the part of a staff member or a fellow performer, but if you are being mistreated in any way, you need to tell someone.

Discrimination may include being fired because of your age, or not being hired based on your race. Federal law states that it is illegal for an employer to discriminate against someone on the basis of race, color, religion, sex (including pregnancy), national origin, age (forty or older), disability, or genetic health information. If you feel that you are being discriminated against for any of these reasons and you are a union employee, you should absolutely speak to a union official about the situation. Your union can help you to determine whether you should take your complaint further and, if so, what you need to do. If you are not a union employee, you can seek help from the U.S. Equal Employment Opportunity Commission (www.eeoc.gov), the agency that is responsible for enforcing federal discrimination laws. On the website they have, among other tools, an online self-assessment system that can help you to decide if pursuing a claim through the EEOC would be your best course of action. Once you complete the questionnaire, you can either mail it or take it to one of the EEOC's field offices, of which there are fifty-three across the country. Keep in mind, however, that you *can* be fired for things that you might feel are unfair (such as if your boss thinks you are lazy or rude or that you are not a team player) but are not protected by law. You may disagree, and it may not be nice, but it is not legally discrimination.

Harassment in the workplace is a different kettle of fish, and while most people equate the term specifically with unwanted sexual advances, it can also be based on the protected characteristics listed above, such as the use of derogatory ethnic or religious terms or age- or disability-related comments. These bad behaviors must, however, be consistent and repetitive enough to show a pattern of abuse that is sufficient to create a hostile environment that interferes with your work. That said, the most talked-about form of harassment is still, in fact, sexual.

According to the EEOC website:

Sexual harassment includes unwelcome sexual advances, requests for sexual favors, and verbal or physical conduct of a sexual nature when:

* **Engaging in such conduct is made an implicit or explicit term or condition of employment.** Example: A newly hired machine operator is told sexual jokes, touching, and display of nude posters are just part of factory life and she should try to ignore it.
* **Acceptance or rejection of such conduct is used as the basis for an employment decision affecting an employee.** Example: A manager tells a worker applying for a promotion that the job would be his if he just "treated her right."

* The conduct interferes with an employee's work or creates an intimidating, hostile, or offensive work environment. Example: One worker experiences repeated advances from another asking her for dates or "just to go out for drinks after work." The worker says she isn't interested, but the coworker won't take "no" for an answer.

Whether it's a colleague or a supervisor who's doing the abusing, no one has to allow him- or herself (and, yes, men, too, can be sexually harassed) to be either physically or verbally assaulted in any way. And yes, I know, *assault* is a strong word, but when you're on the receiving end of an unpleasant encounter, that's what it is, and, moreover, what it feels like.

Do keep in mind, though, not all bad behavior is technically harassment or illegal. Just because your boss is "nasty" or rude to you does not mean it is harassment; it just means that he or she is a jerk. No one has to work for a jerk, and that will be a decision you will possibly need to make at various points in your career, but being a jerk is not illegal. Part of learning to navigate your career will be based on deciding whom you do or do not want to work for, and what opportunities a particular job might bring. Over the years there have been notoriously callous, rude, and infuriating directors, teachers, choreographers, and conductors who have also been great artists. It will be up to you to weigh your options and opportunities and determine whether or not working for or with one of these individuals is worth it to you. This is your personal calculus and no one else's. Some performers don't let the rude and mean get to them; others are crushed by it. You have to make that call.

DEALING WITH ADDICTION AND NUTRITION

I'm sure many people will find it odd that I'm putting addiction and nutrition in the same category, but, certainly in the performing arts world, stress can—and too often does—lead to the abuse of drugs and/or alcohol as well as the abuse of food. Abusing any of these three substances simply means that you're consuming them incorrectly—in the case of drugs or drink by consuming too much, and in the case of food either too little or too much. Either way, if you think you recognize yourself in this picture, you need help.

We've already talked about nerves and stage fright, and both drugs and alcohol can help to take the edge off. The problem is that, not unlike debt, substance abuse can creep up on you while you're not looking. One drink makes you feel good, so surely another one will make you feel even better. Same with drugs—one mood elevator calms the nerves and peps you up. But after the show you're still raring to go, so maybe a tranquilizer will help you get to sleep—until, that is, you need to be up early for class or rehearsal, and so another upper couldn't hurt. Before you know it, you're trapped in a vicious cycle. And I'm not even talking about recreational drugs here—these are all prescription meds that can be really helpful when they're taken properly. Add injury to the equation and pain meds also become more tempting than they should be.

As for nutrition, or food, working hard—running as fast as you can—virtually all day every day, can easily lead to skipping meals here and there, or grabbing something on the fly. And, of course, if you're in a field, such as dance, where thin is in and thinner often seems to be better, it might seem like a good thing to eat less and less, or, if you're starving, to binge and then purge. For dancers in particular—but also for any performer who buys into the unrealistic standards of thinness our society equates with beauty—anorexia, bulimia, or disordered eating are dangers always lurking just around the corner.

What you need to appreciate is that no employer wants to invest time and money in someone who isn't healthy and, as a result, can't keep up, may not show up, and is often ill or injured. Any company (because remember, this is, at root, a business) is looking for employees who are healthy and who know how to stay healthy—which can be harder than it looks. Learning to manage your time so you can maintain your health is not easy, and the habits you develop early in your career can have lifelong implications.

At ABT, when a dancer has a problem with substance abuse, he or she is referred to the Actors Fund, which offers high-quality addiction and recovery services and is an invaluable resource for the performing arts community (http://www.actorsfund.org /services-and-programs/addiction-and-recovery-services).

Similarly, the Los Angeles Philharmonic has an Employee Assistance Plan that offers counseling services through an organization called Empathia, which provides highly customized behavior, health, and emergency programs. The orchestra also travels with a doctor when they tour to assist musicians who may have medical challenges.

For nutrition questions or eating disorders, ABT recommends the high-quality team of nutritionists at Brown & Medina Nutrition (www.brownmedinanutrition.com), who have a long history of working with athletes and performing artists of all types. If you are looking for a nutritionist in your area, try to find one who has worked with athletes or other people who have to "manage performance." A knowledgeable nutritionist can help you to formulate a diet that will maximize your performance onstage or in the studio.

In the end, if your life is being negatively impacted by the misuse of alcohol, drugs, or food, you need to get treatment. Counseling, therapy, or other expert advice can help you manage your challenges and get healthy so that you are able to become a more successful artist with a sustained career.

TROUBLE WITH THE IRS (OR, NOTHING IS CERTAIN IN LIFE BUT DEATH AND TAXES)

Doing tax returns and making all your payments in a timely fashion can be complicated and time consuming. In Chapter 6, we discussed many of the issues involved with income taxes in a variety of employment situations, and suggested when it might be advisable to pay a professional to help you get it right. The problem is that, if things go wrong, the consequences can haunt you for years. But if you do get in trouble with the IRS, there are places to turn for help.

One such resource is the Taxpayer Advocate Service (www.taxpayeradvocate.irs.gov), an independent organization within the IRS that works with taxpayers to resolve issues they have not been able to fix on their own. The TAS tackles about 250,000 cases each year. More than half the cases they deal with involve taxpayers who are suffering financial hardship because of their tax issues, and they are generally able to provide relief for three-quarters of those who come to them or help.

Another resource for low-income individuals is the Low Income Taxpayer Clinics (www.irs.gov/advocate)—which are separate, but receive grant money from the IRS—that advocate for and help low-income taxpayers with audits, appeals, collection disputes, and other problems at low or no cost. It is up to the LITC to determine whether prospective clients meet the guidelines for eligibility before agreeing to represent them. A list of all LITCs is available at your local IRS office.

KNOWING YOUR RIGHTS AS A RENTER

The lease on an apartment is a legal document, and your rent will probably be your greatest expense, so you need to take it seriously and know both your rights and obligations.

Read the terms of your lease. What are the dates of the lease? Does the rent increase during the term of the lease? What are the terms for a security deposit? Do you get it back when you move out if there is little or no damage to the apartment? How long will it take to get that money back? In some states, the landlord is required to put your security deposit into a separate account and actually send you the interest at the end of every year.

One particular issue that impacts many performers is the ability to sublet. When I was dancing at ABT, we toured for months at a time. In a typical year, we would leave New York City in January and not return until late April or May. You certainly don't want to be paying rent on an apartment you won't be living in for several months of the year, and that's where the question of subletting comes in. Does your lease state that you are able to sublet, and, if so, what are the terms? Does it mention subletting at all? If it doesn't, or even if it says that subletting is not allowed, call and ask your landlord. Even if your current lease says "no," he might be willing to make an exception if you explain your situation and the sublet seems reasonable.

If you are going to sublet:

* Get an agreement in writing that is signed by you, the person to whom you are subletting, and your landlord. Your landlord may already have a form you can use; otherwise, do a Web search for "sublet agreement (name of state)" to find one that is legally binding.
* Get a security deposit, generally one month's rent, and make sure your agreement states that if your subtenant damages the premises or fails to pay the rent on time, you will keep the deposit to offset your costs.
* Protect your deposit and belongings (if you are subletting a furnished space) with a walk-through inspection both before the subtenant takes occupancy and at the end of the sublease. During the initial walk-through, take photos to confirm the condition of the space and the furnishings.
* Remove your personal items and store them at a friend's house or in a small storage unit, which you can rent by the month.
* If you have roommates, be sure to involve them in the search for a subtenant. They have a right to know and to help choose the person with whom they will be living.

* In terms of rates, you can try to charge the full amount you pay for rent, but don't be surprised if you don't get it. If you get 70 to 80 percent of your current rent, you should feel good about the deal. Of course, you can charge whatever you can get, but this is a good baseline.

Sublet Insecurity

In the fall of 2012 my friend Dana and her husband rented their Los Angeles house to another family for six months because Dana's husband was going to be appearing in a Broadway show on the East Coast.

Because the people to whom they rented were friends of friends, they thought, as Dana put it, that they had "won the lotto" and were leaving their home in good hands. Although they removed most of their clothing and decorative items, they left the furniture and the majority of kitchenware.

The only two stipulations in their lease agreement were:

1. No smokers
2. Pets in the backyard only; not in the front

As it turned out, "Grandma," who was acting as the children's nanny, was a smoker (although they didn't know that until they got back). True, she didn't smoke in the house, but the smell of smoke on her clothing and her person permeated Dana's daughters' room, where she was sleeping.

In addition, the family's two dogs were shown on the external surveillance cameras (meant for security, not for spying) running around the front yard, jumping into the koi pond (luckily the koi were with a friend for safekeeping), and then running through the house.

Dana and her husband had left their crib for the renters' one-year-old child to use, and when they got back, it was badly scratched and full of tooth marks. Their own dresser was also very scratched up and the bed frame was nicked. The wood floors were damaged, apparently from the toddler's dragging around a fire poker (which was also broken).

The sheer curtains in the dining and living rooms had been shredded by the dogs, and the icing on the cake was that the tenants took a variety of items, including Dana's dog bowls, a cutting board, knives, can openers, and other kitchen items, when they vacated the premises.

The most serious damage was to the sump pump, which had to be replaced at a cost of $1,000, because it had been stopped up with dental floss and even a disposable diaper flushed down the toilet.

The house was filthy, even though the tenants claimed to have had it cleaned.

When Dana and her husband confronted them, they refused to pay for any of the damage until Dana threatened to take them to court. In the end, they settled, but Dana also learned a hard lesson.

If she ever does sublet again, she will be certain to remove *all* of her belongings. She will absolutely require a security deposit, and she will also be sure the agreement states that the tenants are responsible for any damage they incur.

To me, the moral of this story is that, even if your renter is a friend of a friend, even if you've been to his or her house or apartment, you never know how he'll treat your home. Some people treat other people's property better than their own, while others just don't care. So don't take any chances you don't have to.

APARTMENT REPAIRS

While there are many wonderful and honorable landlords, there are also those who do not live up to their obligations. Tenants do have rights, and if you feel that yours have been violated, you should take action.

For many, the biggest issue is that the landlord does not make necessary repairs. When you move in, be sure to get the landlord's (or management company's) name, address, and phone number. Find out whom you should contact for repairs. If there is a problem, tell the landlord or management company as soon as possible, and ask when you can expect the work to be done. Always put your request in writing, even if you have already spoken in person or on the phone. Be sure to put all your contact information (name, address, telephone, and email) and the date on the letter. Keep a copy of the letter in case you later need to prove that you made the request.

If the repairs are relatively minor, you may want to make them yourself. Or, if you've made a request and the repair isn't done within a reasonable amount of time, you can inform the landlord—in writing of course—that if the work isn't done by a particular date you intend to either do it yourself or hire someone to do it and deduct the cost from your next month's rent. Keep all your receipts and bear in mind that the costs should be reasonable. You should not try to make money on this situation; just get the repairs done. Then, when you do pay your rent, include a letter explaining the work you had done, why, and how much it cost. Send copies of the letter, your receipts, and, if possible, before-and-after photos to your landlord. If there is further trouble, you will need to have good records of your activities.

When the required repair is serious—such as a leak or a heating or plumbing problem—you may need to call the local housing authority. Check with your city, village, or town clerk for more details. In the worst case, you may need to go to court. Contact a local legal aid society to see if they can help with this process. Don't go to court without some kind of legal representation. Dealing with the legal system can be expensive and time consuming, so be sure you know what you are in for before you go down that road.

TROUBLE WHEN YOU TRAVEL ABROAD

When you go abroad to tour or gig, things can happen. If you are robbed, have your passport stolen, or need serious medical assistance, especially in a country where you do not speak the language, you may feel at a loss with nowhere to turn. Actually, this is almost never the case; you do have a friend in almost every country, and that is your U.S. embassy or consulate. If you are in serious trouble, go to www.usembassy.gov to find the embassy or consulate nearest you. These people are trained to help you, so don't be afraid to reach out. If you're going someplace that is out of the way or in a location where there might be national unrest, you may want to register in the State Department's Smart Traveler Enrollment Program, or STEP. This is a free service that allows U.S. citizens and nationals to register with the local U.S. embassy or consulate in advance in order to receive alerts in case of a natural disaster or if safety conditions in the country change, and to help your family and friends get

in touch with you in an emergency. To find out more go to www
.step.state.gov/step.

MANAGING TRAFFIC VIOLATIONS

Unless you live in an urban area with good public transportation, chances are that you'll be driving yourself to gigs, classes,
rehearsals, and performances. When you're driving a lot, you are
more likely to be stopped at some point for some kind of traffic
violation. While this may seem like nothing more than a nui-
sance to you, you do need to take traffic tickets seriously and
handle them expeditiously.

The first thing you need to do is decide whether to fight it
or just pay up. The fines and requirements will vary depending upon where you committed the violation and what type of
violation it is. There's a big difference, for example, between
a parking ticket and a speeding ticket or a ticket for driving
without insurance. Depending upon the violation you could
face:

* Action against your license
* Points on your driving record
* Having to appear in traffic court
* Increased car insurance rates
* Mandatory traffic school

(Please note that parking tickets generally do not have any
effect on the status of your driver's license or on your car
insurance rates.)

Paying Your Ticket

If you choose to pay your ticket (rather than fighting it), do it promptly, because the amount of the fine will increase if you fail to pay before the deadline. Not only that, but if you neglect paying long enough, you could have your license suspended or revoked. Also, be aware that a lost ticket does not excuse you from paying your fine. You are responsible for contacting the traffic court (sometimes this can be done online) and responding to the ticket.

Fighting Your Ticket

If you believe you received a ticket in error or have grounds for contesting the citation, you should plead not guilty to the offense and fight the ticket in court. You may find information about fighting a ticket on the back of the citation you received. Or you can contact the traffic court handling your ticket for more information. Depending on the severity of the situation, you may want to consider hiring a traffic ticket attorney. If the court finds you not guilty, you will avoid the fine and points on your driving record.

IF YOU LOSE YOUR CREDIT CARD

There is nothing quite like the sinking feeling you get when you discover that you have lost a credit card. It's similar to the panic you feel when you discover that you've lost your cell phone, or a shopping bag full of purchases, or even your prescription sunglasses. The difference is that none of those losses can become someone else's opportunity to go on a free shopping spree.

If it happens to you, don't panic. Thankfully, federal law caps your total liability for a stolen or lost credit card at just $50, and many credit card companies have a zero-liability policy that keeps you off the hook for even a single cent.

Call your credit card company *at once*. If you report the lost card before it's been used, you won't have any liability at all; if someone has already made a purchase (or purchases) you may be in for a $50 fee. But beyond that, the sooner you report the loss, the sooner you'll receive your replacement card. Follow up your call with a letter, and keep a copy in your file.

A different problem may arise if your card is right there in your wallet but someone is still making purchases with it. The fact is that people can get your credit card number and use it without ever having the actual card. For that reason, it's important that you examine your bills carefully and immediately report any purchase you don't recognize.

The rules for a lost debit card are a bit different. If you report it within two business days after it goes missing, your liability is $50. However, if you miss the two-day window but report it within 60 days of receiving your next bill, your liability shoots up to $500. And if you wait longer than 60 days, you may be liable for *all* unauthorized purchases.

IT'S NOT WHAT HAPPENS;
IT'S HOW YOU HANDLE IT

Annoying, depressing, scary, challenging, and unfair things happen to everyone. You will probably not be the exception. What you need to remember is that "this too shall pass," and it isn't a sign that you're unlucky or are walking around with a little rain cloud over your head.

As both an artist and a human being, you are going to be judged not on the fact that something went wrong or you hit a stumbling block but on your ability to manage the problem and improve the situation, whatever it might be.

I remember seeing the movie *Apollo 13*, which chronicled the ill-fated space flight in 1970 when one of the liquid oxygen tanks aboard the spaceship exploded and it seemed that there would not be enough oxygen or electricity to get the men home. NASA flight director Gene Kranz didn't panic; he didn't despair. Rather, he took charge and uttered four memorable words: "Work the problem, people." Ultimately, NASA and the astronauts did "work the problem" and the astronauts got home. Kranz's brilliance rested in his understanding that your finest hour most often occurs when you face and are able to overcome a seemingly insurmountable problem.

As I keep saying, artists are some of the most creative and determined problem solvers in the world. If you focus, and "work the problem," I believe you will be able to overcome most of the challenges life throws your way.

Chapter Eight

How to Make a "Life"
(Not Just a Living) as a Performer

You Are More Than What You Do for a Living

Happiness is not a matter of intensity
but of balance, order, rhythm, and harmony.

—THOMAS MERTON

Although, up to this point, we've talked a bit about creating a balance and taking care of yourself, we have mainly been concentrating on the skills you'll need to succeed in the business of the performing arts. Before I leave you, though, I want to be sure you understand that being "successful" involves finding pleasure in every aspect of your life—off stage as well as on. While it's certainly hard to have a happy and meaningful life if you can't earn a living, it's equally difficult to enjoy life if all you do is work.

Sadly, looking across all aspects of the performing arts, one sees many wonderful performers who leave the field simply because they are unable to sustain themselves. They burn out, get injured, or become dispirited by their "lack of success." This is incredibly unfortunate for both the performer and the field. Why? Because these individuals have spent many years and a great deal of money seeking to attain a certain level of training; they have dedicated their lives to the creation of great art, and for them to leave the field prematurely is not only a tragedy for them personally, but also for their art, which loses the benefit of their skill, wisdom, and perspective.

To prevent that from happening to you, I am hoping to provide you with some tools and strategies that will help you to build a sustainable artistic life. As you move through your career, you will be faced with many choices. I hope that, over time, you will think long-term and make decisions that serve you well as a creative professional.

YOU ARE MORE THAN YOUR WORK

When you are just starting out, it probably seems okay to immerse yourself in your art form, shutting out the rest of the world and working twenty-six hours a day, eight days a week. The problem is that you cannot last that way, *and* it's not necessarily the best way to create the greatest art.

So how do you create that all-important balance?

1. **Carve out pockets of time for friends and family.** Those who care about you, and whom you trust, can be the ones to lift your sprits when you're down and keep you grounded when you're about to fly off into space without a safety net. It's important to have people around you who know you as something other than

a performing artist. They bring a perspective to your life that goes beyond that of professional colleagues, competitors, and teachers.

2. Limit time-wasting people and activities. Many people waste time involving themselves with others who add no value to their lives. For instance, you can get stuck spending a lot of time speaking with colleagues who are venting and gossiping or those who expect you to drop everything to attend to them because they think their needs and their careers are more important than yours. This takes precious time and energy away from your important work as an artist. I recommend that you limit your availability to people who have a negative view of the world. As Cenovia Cummins has noted, you need to exude positive energy (even when you don't want to), and surrounding yourself with people who are negative can be corrosive to your spirit.

Besides being thoughtful about your personal and professional relationships, you may simply want to make a conscious effort to limit the time you spend on activities that really just take up time. Monitor the time you spend on social media, texting, or surfing the Web. Try keeping a log of your activities for a week or a month. I think you will be surprised to find how you really use your time, as opposed to how you *think* you use your time. It is easy to get sucked into habits that make you less efficient without even realizing it.

3. Build some real downtime into your schedule. In addition to the time you spend with family and friends, schedule some time to relax by yourself. What is it that allows your mind to rest? Yoga? Reading a book? Taking a walk? Taking a nap? Watching a movie or television program? Scheduling some time to rest your mind will actually make you more productive. Even during a hectic day, you can take ten or fifteen minutes to recharge your batteries. You have to make a little time to let your mind and body rest, and you will be much more effective for having done so.

4. Take the time to explore other art forms or new experiences. Broadening your range of experience enriches you not only as a human being but also as an artist. In the ballet world, there used to be a prevailing if misguided belief that young artists should spend all their time in the studio or on the stage. Broadening one's worldview and learning about things outside the ballet world, was frowned upon. It was felt that those who explored the "outside world" would be distracted or, even worse, not regarded as truly dedicated to their art form.

Happily, this notion no longer prevails, because it is patently false and incredibly unproductive. Performers need to understand the world around them in order to enrich themselves as artists who bring depth and meaning to their work. How much more effectively might you perform in *Romeo and Juliet* after knowing the overwhelming thrill of first love? How much more meaning would you bring to playing Elgar's Cello Concerto in E Minor if you yourself had known heartbreak and pain? What new depth would the loss of a loved one bring to your dancing Martha Graham's *Lamentation*? How can you perform *La Bohème* if you don't understand the social, historical, or cultural background of the time period within which it is set? An educated, intellectually curious, and knowledgeable artist is invariably a richer artist, one who has the ability not only to bring more to his or her art but also to have a more personally meaningful experience in the process.

5. Look beyond the major cities for your career. Having a meaningful artistic career does not necessarily require you to live in a big, expensive city. For some, building a sustainable existence means *not* living in New York or Los Angeles, but in a smaller community where the cost of living is lower and the stress of city life is less. If you look around the United States, you can find great art being made in communities of all sizes. From Minneapolis–St. Paul, Minnesota, to Portland, Oregon, to Austin, Texas, there are many vibrant artistic centers. Open your horizons and you may find that, for you, a balanced and sustainable existence can be made outside a mega-metropolis.

6. Work smart, not hard. Performers are generally high-performing, driven perfectionists. This is good, except when it isn't. Learning to be strategic is key. As we discussed earlier, you need to be smart about where you put your effort. Learn to say "no" to a project that doesn't advance your career or pay well enough to satisfy your practical needs.

7. Take care of your body. Whether you are a dancer, singer, actor, or musician, a healthy body is critical to the execution of sustainable quality work.

Eat well.

I know it sounds counterintuitive, but many performers, despite the fact that they are so dependent upon having a healthy body, do not know how or what to eat to fuel it properly. We've talked about the prevalence of eating disorders, particularly among those who struggle to meet an almost impossible level of leanness, but there's really more to it than that. Your body needs a balance of various nutrients to function at its best—which means protein to keep you feeling full, complex carbohydrates for the antioxidants that keep you healthy, and good fats (yes, there are good fats) for cellular integrity, among other things. If you have any doubts about the efficacy of your own diet, do visit with a nutritionist who can guide you. As I mentioned earlier, ABT often works with Brown & Medina, but there are many good nutritionists throughout the country who specialize in working with high-performance individuals.

Exercise.

And that means everyone, including dancers. Most people assume that dancers couldn't possibly need more exercise than they're already getting day in and day out. However, professional dancers should do some cross-training and cardio work to improve stamina and prevent injury. By working with a physical therapist, dancers can learn about their weak spots and do preventive training to limit the likelihood of injury. For instance, we often see highly trained dancers who have overstrengthened some muscle groups and underworked others. That kind of imbalance can lead to injury. In fact, it is essential for all dancers to work with a physical therapist and be disciplined about their training, especially on tour, when rigorous classes may be difficult to find and their regular training regime is disrupted.

For everyone else, exercise will keep you healthier. And, as with dancers, this is particularly important when you go on tour. Difficult travel schedules and limited access to healthy food may make you want to skip exercise. But this, of course, is when you need it most. When I was touring with ABT, I—along with many others—struggled to maintain an optimal level of fitness. At the time, most hotels did not have gyms or places to work out, do Pilates, or even practice yoga. The result was that we returned to New York needing to "get back into shape." Nowadays, access to exercise equipment, videos, and biking or walking trails is much more prevalent. Use them. If you can keep fit, you will probably be much more productive, perform at a higher level, and stay healthier over time.

I am not suggesting that you need to be a triathlete, but regular exercise has innumerable benefits and will keep you in top competitive form.

Studies have shown that regular exercise reduces stress and the physical manifestations of stress (sleeping poorly, high blood pressure, high cholesterol). It also helps to strengthen the immune system to fight off or recover more quickly from the occasional cold or flu bug we all experience from time to time. Anyone whose goal is to perform at their highest level knows that no one does their best work when they're coughing or sneezing.

Sleep.

The majority of people need between seven and eight hours of sleep to function at their best, and most adults in the United States do not get enough. According to Dr. Lisa Shives, medical director of Northshore Sleep Medicine, "I think an hour less a night consistently is enough to see impairment in people's cognition and mood." And, she adds, "there are those that can function on five hours of sleep, but that's five percent of the population," and there are still questions about their level of performance. Pilots are not allowed to fly and truck drivers can't drive when they haven't had enough sleep. That ought to tell you something about the relationship between sleep and performance.

I know you may be thinking, "I don't have enough time in the day to squeeze in all my activities as it is. How could I possibly spend any more time asleep?" But you need to find that time, because lack of sleep, in addition to affecting your mood and ability to think clearly, has also been shown to affect your metabolism. Lack of sleep leads to overeating, which leads to weight gain, which leads to binge dieting, which leads to all kinds of mental and physical problems. Shakespeare was right (as usual) when he referred to sleep as

. . . *sore labor's bath,*
Balm of hurt minds, great nature's second course,
Chief nourisher in life's feast.

—*Macbeth*, Act II, Scene 2

And if you're counting on a couple of cans of Red Bull or multiple cups of coffee to get you through the day, I'm here to tell you that you're just asking for trouble down the road.

So go to bed!

YOUR WORK IS IMPORTANT

There will be days when you are afraid. When you are tired. When you are dispirited. Before you give up, please keep in mind that the arts are important, that you are important. Circling back to the beginning, I noted that the world needs the arts. Your unique voice and your worldview are critical. The world needs to see itself in new and different ways. The arts do not only express great emotion; they also help us to better understand and experience the world around us. So, in those dark days, remember that your work is essential to our culture, our community, and our world.

Parting Words from Sigourney Weaver

- Enjoy the path. Enjoy the journey.
- Forgive abusive teachers. Forgive yourself for putting up with the abuse.
- Your job is stay in really good shape physically and emotionally, especially if you want longevity in this business.
- Be resourceful.

MY WISH FOR YOU

What I wish for everyone in the arts business is for them to create a high-performing and sustainable lifestyle. If you truly have something important to say with your art, the more years you have to work, the better for you as an artist and for the world, which will benefit from the beauty, honesty, and creativity of your vision.

Despite the beautiful words of the poet Edna St. Vincent Millay—

> *My candle burns at both ends;*
> *It will not last the night;*
> *But ah, my foes, and oh, my friends—*
> *It gives a lovely light!*

—flameout is not a goal to which anyone should aspire. No one wants to be a flash in the pan, a precocious star who burns brightly and then disappears.

My hope is that, with the help of this book, and with people who guide and care for you, you will have a long and bright career and a joyful life.

Bibliography

Beeching, Angela Miles. *Beyond Talent: Creating a Successful Career in Music*. New York: Oxford University Press, 2010.

Conner, Cheryl Snapp. "Mentally Strong People: The 13 Things They Avoid." *Forbes*, November 18, 2013.

Horowitz, Sara, and Toni Sciarra Poynter. *The Freelancer's Bible*. New York: Workman, 2012.

Kane, Susan Mohini. *The 21st-Century Singer*. New York: Oxford University Press, 2015.

Krasilovsky, M. William, and Sidney Shemel. *The Business of Music: The Definitive Guide to the Business and Legal Issues of the Music Industry*. New York: Billboard Books, 2003.

LearnVest. *The Face of Personal Finance: A LearnVest and Chase Blueprint® Study*. Study conducted in 2012. http://www .learnvest.com/wp-content/uploads/2011/03/100912_white -paper.pdf (downloaded December 23, 2013).

Letts, Quentin. "The Terror That Turns Our Acting Giants to Jelly." *DailyMail.com*, August 27, 2013. http://www.dailymail .co.uk/tvshowbiz/article-2403635/Quentin-Letts-Stage-fright -Laurence-Olivier-Benedict-Cumberbatch-Michael-Gambon .html.

Pomfret, Emma. "Lang Lang: China's Classical Superstar." *Times*, April 11, 2009.

Simonet, Andrew. *Making Your Life as an Artist*. Artists U, 2014.

Young, Robin, and Jeremy Hobson. "How to Start Conversations with Total Strangers." *Here & Now*, WBUR Radio, April 14, 2014.

Further Reading

The books below will provide you with additional information on some of the most important aspects of building and managing your career in the performing arts.

Branding and Career Development

Artspire. *The Profitable Artist: A Handbook for All Artists in the Performing, Literary, and Visual Arts*. New York: Allworth Press, 2011.
The New York Foundation for the Arts (nyfa.org) has been providing essential services to artists of all disciplines since 1971. This book provides a "best practices" approach to planning and organizing a career in the arts.

Clark, Dorie. *Reinventing You: Define Your Brand, Imagine Your Future*. Boston: Harvard Business Review Press, 2013.
Clark is a branding expert who offers a step-by-step plan for defining the unique qualities that will set you apart from the crowd.

Jahnke, Christine K. *The Well-Spoken Woman: Your Guide to Looking and Sounding Your Best*. Amherst, NY: Prometheus Books, 2011.

Jahnke, a well-known speech coach, will help you to make the best impression at interviews, take the best advantage of networking opportunities, and generally put your best foot forward in every situation.

O'Malley, Michael, and William F. Baker. *Every Leader Is an Artist: How the World's Greatest Artists Can Make You a More Creative Leader.* New York: McGraw-Hill Education, 2012.
O'Malley, a human resource consultant, and Baker, former president of the Educational Broadcasting Corporation, argue that the same traits that make a great artist are also the qualities that make great leaders. To me, this is another way of saying that those who are forward-looking, focused, and in charge of their careers are the artists who are most likely to succeed.

Sandberg, Sheryl. *Lean In: Women, Work, and the Will to Lead.* New York: Knopf, 2013.
The chief operating officer of Facebook talks about how women may unintentionally hold themselves back in their careers. In these changing and competitive times it's more important than ever that women in the performing arts learn how to put themselves forward and become more entrepreneurial in terms of their career development. *Lean In* provides essential information from one who has done it.

Wienir, David, and Jodie Langel. *Making It on Broadway: Actors' Tales of Climbing to the Top.* New York: Allworth Press, 2004.
Get the unvarnished truth about the life of a Broadway performer as more than 150 stars tell their own stories.

Personal Finance and the
Business of the Performing Arts

Benun, Ilise. *The Creative Professional's Guide to Money*. Cincinnati: HOW Books, 2011.

Benun offers a wide range of proven techniques and resources that all creative professionals can use to better manage their business finances.

Brown, Leanne. *Good and Cheap: Eat Well on $4/Day*. New York: Workman, 2015.

Many young artists complain about being unable to afford delicious, healthy food. Leanne Brown's book is a wonderful resource for learning how to nourish your body with healthy food on only four dollars a day.

Hanlon, R. Brendan. *The New Tax Guide for Performers, Writers, Directors, Designers and Other Show Biz Folk*. New York: Limelight Editions, 2004.

Every business has specific tax deductions that will keep more money in the earner's pocket—and that is particularly true for show business. This guide not only provides you with information about those deductions but also tells you how to keep proper records so that the legal deductions you take won't be questioned or disallowed.

Leland, Caryn R. *Licensing Art & Design: A Professional's Guide to Licensing and Royalty Agreements*. New York: Allworth Press, 1995.

Whether you're licensing your own work—for example, as a photographer—or would like to use someone else's, Leland provides the legal expertise you need to be sure all the loopholes are closed and the deal is on the up-and-up.

McLaughlin, Thomas A. *Streetsmart Financial Basics for Non-profit Managers*. Hoboken, NJ: Wiley, 2009.

Even though you may not be in a position to start your own nonprofit at this point in your career, you will still benefit from knowing how a nonprofit arts organization is managed—especially since many of you will likely be working for one.

Stim, Richard. *Getting Permission: How to License & Clear Copyrighted Materials Online & Off*. Berkeley, CA: NOLO, 2013.

Attorney Stim takes you through the ins and outs of getting permission to use copyrighted material.

Acknowledgments

I would like to thank the countless people who believed in me and helped me over the years. I especially want to thank those whose insights, advice, and generosity of time and spirit made this book possible, in particular Mona Metwalli, for encouraging me to move forward on what seemed an impossible task, and Toddi Gutner, who introduced me to her incredible agent, Susan Ginsburg. Susan believed in this project straightaway and has been a constant source of invaluable counsel through a process that, for someone not from the publishing world, was completely nerve-racking.

To Elaine Wilson and Michelle Howry of Simon & Schuster, whose enthusiasm for this project was overwhelming. I am grateful for their patience and extraordinary guidance.

To my amazing husband, Robert Ryan. His emotional support was unconditional and his patience was limitless.

I am so thankful for all the brilliant minds, generous hearts, and candid conversations of the performers, administrators, and arts professionals I interviewed for this book. Without you, it would not exist. Thank you, William Baker, Dana Stackpole Barbour, Kristin Arnold Bell, Shelly Berc, Celeste Billeci, Deborah Borda, Siobhan Burke, Yvette Campbell, Laura Careless, Jean Jacques Cebron, Cenovia Cummins, Peter Diggins, Terry Dwyer, Jennifer Edwards, Teresa Eyring, James Fayette, Amy Fitterer, Renée Fleming, James Gandry, Adam Gwon, Adam Huttler, Jordan Isadore, Christopher Koelsch, Julia Levy, Nigel Lythgoe, Rosa Lamoreaux, David LaMarche, Lang Lang, Sharon Luckman, Michael Mael, David Mallette, Kevin McKenzie, Anya Nykyforiak, Rosalie O'Connor, Victoria Phillips, Linda Shelton, Daniil Simkin, Sydney Skybetter, Ken Tabachnick, Sigourney Weaver, John Weidman, Ormsby Wilkins, and Francesca Zambello.

Many thanks to the family, friends, and colleagues who supported me, cheered me on, and believed in me throughout this process: Madeline Eckett Oden, Lorraine Shanley, Carl Liederman, Patricia Francy, Katharine Moore, Anna Moore, Ernestine Miller, Bruce Moore, and Cathy Moore.

Thanks to David Lansky, Emily Waters, and James Timm for their help and support on this project.

Finally, a special thanks to Judy Kern, whose help and support were invaluable, and whose candor and sense of humor helped make the journey a pleasure.

Index

INDEX

Rachel S. Moore was named president and CEO of The Music Center in 2015. A former member of American Ballet Theatre's *corps de ballet*, Moore was named executive director of ABT in April 2004 and CEO in 2012. Prior to her appointment, she served as director of Boston Ballet's Center for Dance Education; as executive director of Project STEP, a classical music school for students of color in Boston; and as managing director of Ballet Theatre of Boston. She has also held senior positions with Americans for the Arts and the National Cultural Alliance, both in Washington, DC.

She currently serves as a trustee of the Economic Club of New York, a member of the advisory committee of the Dizzy Feet Foundation, and an advisor of Project STEP. Moore holds a bachelor's degree from Brown University (Phi Beta Kappa, honors, 1992) and a master's in arts administration from Columbia University (1994). A native of Davis, California, her father was an economist at the University of California at Davis and her mother was actively involved in Davis public service, so Moore spent much of her early childhood living abroad with her family in India and Saudi Arabia. As a teenager, she spent summers in New York City and trained on scholarship at the School of American Ballet and American Ballet Theatre School before becoming a professional ballet dancer. She currently lives in Los Angeles with her husband, two Labradors, and cats of suspect provenance.